Time Out

TOP 100
CHEAP
EATS

www.timeout.com

Time Out Digital Ltd
4th Floor
125 Shaftesbury Avenue
London WC2H 8AD
United Kingdom
Tel: +44 (0)20 7813 3000
Fax: +44 (0)20 7813 6001
Email: guides@timeout.com
www.timeout.com

Published by Time Out Digital Ltd, a wholly owned subsidiary of Time Out Group Ltd.
Time Out and the Time Out logo are trademarks of Time Out Group Ltd.

© **Time Out Group Ltd 2013**

10 9 8 7 6 5 4 3

This edition first published in Great Britain in 2013 by Ebury Publishing
20 Vauxhall Bridge Road, London SW1V 2SA

Ebury Publishing is part of the Penguin Random House group of companies whose addresses
can be found at global.penguinrandomhouse.com

Distributed in the US and Latin America by Publishers Group West (1-510-809-3700)

For further distribution details, see www.timeout.com

ISBN: 978-1-84670-213-6

A CIP catalogue record for this book is available from the British Library.

Printed and bound in India by Replika Press Pvt. Ltd.

Penguin Random House is committed to a sustainable future for our business, our readers and
our planet. This book is made from Forest Stewardship Council® certified paper.

MIX
Paper from
responsible sources
FSC® C018179

Editorial
Editor Sarah Guy
Deputy Editor Cath Phillips
Researcher Olivia Rye
Proofreader John Watson

Editorial Director Sarah Guy
Management Accountant
    Margaret Wright

Design
Senior Designer Kei Ishimaru
Senior Designer (Commercial)
    Jason Tansley

Picture Desk
Picture Editor Jael Marschner
Picture Researcher Ben Rowe

Advertising
Sales Director St John Betteridge
Account Managers Deborah Maclaren, Bobbie
Kelsall-Freeman @ The Media Sales House

Marketing
Senior Publishing Brand Manager
    Luthfa Begum
Head of Circulation Dan Collins

Production
Production Editor Dave Faulkner
Production Controller Katie Mulhern-Bhudia

Time Out Group
Director & Founder Tony Elliott
Chief Executive Officer Aksel Van der Wal
Editor-in-Chief Tim Arthur
UK Chief Commercial Officer David Pepper
Time Out International Ltd MD Cathy Runciman
Group IT Director Simon Chappell
Group Marketing Director Carolyn Sims

Contributors
Tania Ballantine, Dorothy Bourne, Simon Coppock, Guy Dimond, Sarah Guy, Ronnie Haydon-Jones, Anna Norman, Cath Phillips, Celia Plender, Olivia Rye, and reviewers from the Time Out London Eating & Drinking Guide.

Cover photography Rob Greig.

Photography pages 3, 7 (bottom left), 32, 33, 34/35, 79, 80, 81, 110, 143 (top right) Tricia De Courcy Ling; pages 6, 7 (top right), 17, 23, 38, 29, 49 (bottom), 52, 53, 58, 59, 64/65, 74/75, 82 (bottom), 100/101, 114, 115 (bottom), 122, 123, 127, 132, 146 (top), 147 (bottom) Rob Greig; pages 6 (middle), 69 Annie Armitage; pages 7 (top left), 11 (top), 18, 19, 82 (top), 99 Alys Tomlinson; pages 7 (bottom right), 21, 25, 76, 77, 85, 90, 91, 118, 119, 148, 151 Jonathan Perugia; pages 9, 41 (bottom), 48, 60, 61, 62 (top right), 63, 72, 77 (top right), 84, 86, 94, 95, 103, 106, 107, 111, 113, 116, 117, 126, 143, 145, 149 Britta Jaschinski; pages 9 (top), 104, 153 Michael Franke; pages 11 (bottom), 142 David Axelbank; pages 13, 44, 45, 46, 47, 54, 136, 137 Jamie Lau; pages 14, 15 Paul Winch-Furness; pages 20, 24, 27, 31, 37, 40, 41, 93, 96/97, 112, 115 (top) Ed Marshall; pages 39, 55, 56, 57, 66 (bottom), 71, 124/125, 128, 129, 130, 131, 135, 146 (bottom), 152 Jael Marschner; page 43, 88, 89 Michelle Grant; page 49 (top), 147 (top) Kate Peters; pages 50, 120, 121, 133, 134, 141, 144 Ming Tang-Evans; pages 51, 78, 92 Martin Daly; page 59 (top left) Nick Ballon; page 62 (top right), 73, 98, 105 Jitka Hynkova; page 62 (left) Oliver Knight; page 66 (top), 87 Ben Rowe; page 83 Heloise Bergman; page 102 Christina Theisen; pages 108, 109 Thomas Bowles; page 138 Susie Rea; page 139 Kei Ishimaru; page 150 Ben Rowe.

The following images were provided by the featured establishments: pages 67, 68, 140.

Introduction

There has never been a better time to find a good value meal in London. Yes, it can be an expensive place to dine, but if you know where to look, there are plenty of quality meals at wallet-friendly prices.

To help you choose, Top 100 Cheap Eats identifies the pick of the bunch, taking in gourmet street food, foodie hotspots such as Brixton Market, the Indian restaurants and cafés of Wembley, and the last of the retro caffs. Whether you're looking for a £5 set lunch, a gourmet bowl of noodles or the finest hot dog in town, we've got it covered.

FINDING A RESTAURANT
To find restaurants by name, area or cuisine, turn to the indexes starting on p154. To find a restaurant for a specific occasion, try Best for... (p6).

THE LISTINGS
While every effort has been made to ensure the accuracy of the information contained in this guide, the publishers cannot accept responsibility for any errors it may contain. Businesses can change their arrangements at any time, and it is always advisable to phone ahead to check opening hours, prices and other particulars.

TELEPHONE NUMBERS
All telephone numbers listed in this guide assume that you are calling from within London. If you're ringing from outside the city, you will need to use the area code (020) before the phone number. If you're calling from abroad, dial your international access code or a '+', then 44 for the UK; follow that with 20 for London, then the eight-digit number.

WHAT DO YOU THINK?
We welcome feedback on all our guides, so please email any comments or suggestions you may have to guides@timeout.com.

Best for...

The numbers below refer to **page numbers**.

Busaba Eathai

Wardour Street
Store Street
Bird Street
Panton Street
Old Street
Westfield
Shepherd's Bush
Bicester Village
Floral Street
Westfield
Stratford City
King's Road
busaba.com

NIGHTS OUT WITH FRIENDS

WATERSIDE DINING

 Vietnamese Restaurant

Hai Ha was the first Vietnamese Restaurant in Mare Street, Hackney, which opened in 1998. Having recently enjoyed a face lift, including the addition of air-conditioning, Hai Ha offers a modern yet cosy feel with subtle lighting and unfussy furnishing.

The freshest ingredients are used to make your Vietnamese meal truly authentic and our regular customers include Vietnamese natives who appreciate the tastes of our traditional Vietnamese dishes, including the chef's signature Pho which is taken straight from our home kitchens, providing truly amazing flavours from start to finish.

Come to Hai Ha for Vietnamese food at affordable prices. We are the perfect place for your lunch break or casual evening dining and we are now licensed & serving well priced wines and beers. Or simply bring your own (corkage will be charged).

Come and join us for some real Vietnamese Food
Open for Lunch and Dinner

www.haiha.co.uk

206 Mare Street,
Hackney,
London E8 3RD
T: 020 8985 5388

TAKE AWAY & DELIVERY AVAILABLE
Restaurant available for private hire

Top 100
Cheap Eats

1 Roti Chai

The name provides the clue: Roti Chai (bread, tea) is dedicated to serving inexpensive, café-style Indian food. It does so with some panache, in a stylish, contemporary setting. As you enter, you're faced with a counter stocked with colourful packets of Indian produce, and a serving hatch decorated with the vivid primary-coloured hues of retro street-food advertisements (emblazoned with statements such as 'imli pani: finest ingredients'). The menu offers street snacks from across India: from the crisp bhel pooris of Mumbai beaches to Gujarati steamed dokhla (a savoury sponge well matched with coconut chutney). Railway lamb curry is a light, punchy dish with chunks of potatoes, while a Bengali fish curry is pungently flavoured with mustard seeds. A 'dining room' menu contains the likes of chettinad chicken (from Tamil Nadu) and kozhikode seafood curry from Kerala. Service has been a weak link in the past.

3 Portman Mews South, W1H 6HS (7408 0101, www.rotichai.com). Marble Arch tube. Meals served noon-10.30pm Mon-Sat; 1-9pm Sun. Main courses £4.50-£8.50.

2 Counter Café

Counter Cafe retains much from its original boho incarnation up the road – alt-folk sounds, rough floor, tables of recycled wood blocks, and a row of cinema seats – but feels more grown up now it's settled into the River Lea side of the Stour Space gallery. The staff are cool yet charming, but not always efficient. The menu runs from big breakfasts (skinny but flavour-packed sausages, thick rashers, a dense potato cake, glossy scrambled eggs, and a trademark spicy, garlicky mix of tomatoes and white beans) to enticing pies (pork, apple and fennel, say, or moroccan lamb, aubergine and mint). The once superlative view of the Olympic Stadium is much diminished by three-storey prefabs on the far bank, but new folding tables on river-level decking outside are perfect for observing the coots. Expect the place to be busy at weekends, when tapas is served until late, and note that bookings are not accepted before 6pm. Nearby, sister venue Crate Brewery & Pizzeria serves craft beers and stone-baked pizzas (as well as breakfasts and coffees) from the White Building, Queen's Yard, E9 5EN.

Stour Space, 7 Roach Road, E3 2PA (07834 275920, www. thecountercafe.co.uk). Hackney Wick tube/rail or bus 488. Meals served 7.45am-5pm Mon-Fri; 9am-5pm Sat, Sun.

3 Honey & Co

Honey & Co is run by a husband and wife team with an impressive pedigree: Itamar Srulovich (husband) was head chef at Ottolenghi, and Sarit Packer (wife) was both head of pastry at Ottolenghi and executive chef at NOPI. Itamar describes the homely, daily changing menu as 'food from the Middle East'. Dishes are alive with colour and texture. Meze highlights might include beetroot marinated in Corinthian wine vinegar, the tang offset by oregano; or watermelon salad in which sweet, juicy pieces of fruit are a foil to creamy, salty feta, with pistachios, chilli and mint adding crunch, punch and zing. Beautifully textured falafels are exceptional, as is slow-baked lamb shank served with couscous and zhough (a Yemeni spice paste). What this small, plain venue lacks in wall colour, larger-than-life Itamar makes up for tenfold in charm. Tables are hard to come by, so book early. The place is stacked with own-produced comestibles, including the breads and pastries displayed in the window, jars of exotic jams and preserved lemons – but be warned – these are emphatically not a bargain.

25A Warren Street, W1T 5LZ (7388 6175, www.honeyandco. co.uk). Warren Street tube. Meals served 7.30am-6pm Mon; 7.30am-9.30pm Tue-Sat. Main courses £10.50-£15.

4 Jerk City

Jerk City is a simple affair: order food at the counter from a tempting blackboard selection that includes jerk or barbecue chicken, a small range of roti, braised oxtail, brown chicken and huge bowls of soup, and pay with cash. Then grab a seat at a café-style table under the gaze of Barack Obama or one of the Afro-Caribbean hero portraits, and a few minutes later take charge of a huge portion of food, courtesy of the hair-netted cooks from the tiny basement kitchen. All the curries and main meals come with a choice of rice and beans and salad or 'hard' food – plantain, dumpling, yam – and are everything you could hope for. Flaky roti is wrapped around peppery, spicy curry; the hot pepper and herb flavour of chargrilled jerk chicken goes through to the bone; and braised oxtail is a perfect blend of meaty and gloopy. A sweet fresh-fruit punch or a more sedate Guinness punch makes an ideal accompaniment.

189 Wardour Street, W1F 8ZD (7287 2878). Tottenham Court Road tube. Meals served noon-10.30pm Mon-Sat. Main courses £6.50-£9.

5 Itadaki Zen

A Japanese restaurant that's also vegan and organic, Itadaki Zen is a tranquil spot, with frayed tie-dye hessian curtains and bunches of wheat swaying lazily from the ceiling. Despite operating from a narrow pool of ingredients, the predominately noodle/tofu/seaweed menu impresses with its range of tastes and textures. Grilled spring rolls with soft mashed tofu filling make a welcome change from the norm, while 'kakiage' tempura is a wicked golden blend of salty and crisp, served with fluffy rice. All puddings, such as pumpkin cake with tofu cream, are sugar-free, which makes them too savoury for some tastes.

139 King's Cross Road, WC1X 9BJ (7278 3573, www.itadakizen. com). King's Cross tube/rail. Meals served 5.30-9pm Mon-Thur; 5.30-9.30pm Fri, Sat. Set dinner £12.50-£28.

Until you try authentic Neapolitan pizza, you don't know what you're missing. At Rossopomodoro, Italy's favourite pizza restaurant, pizza's made the way it should be – by genuine Neapolitan chefs using the best ingredients delivered directly from Naples. We've been giving value for money in London since 2006 – it's time you tried us!

ROSSOPOMODORO

cucina e pizzeria napoletana

o **Covent Garden** 020 7240 9095 o **Chelsea** 020 7352 7677
o **Notting Hill** 020 7229 9007 o **Hoxton** 020 7739 1899
o **Camden** 020 7424 9900 o **Wandsworth** coming in April

 rossopomodorouk   www.rossopomodoro.co.uk

6 Mandalay

Mandalay's looks – half 'greasy spoon' with brown plastic tablecloths, half Burmese teahouse with wonkily hung pictures of the ancient city of Bagan on the walls – have remained unchanged for years. We wouldn't have it any other way; the place oozes a low-key charm that has garnered it a devoted following. The ten tightly packed tables are full each night. Burma's food draws influence from its bordering countries (India, China and Thailand) and is rendered to a very high standard here, at bargain prices. A tangle of crisp beansprout fritters comes with three dipping sauces: sour tamarind, salty soy and hot chilli. Chicken and shredded cabbage salad has earthy notes of turmeric and caramelised onion. Both meat and vegetarian curries have deeply satisfying flavours and make a hearty meal with rice and naan. A little gem.

444 Edgware Road, W2 1EG (7258 3696, www.mandalayway.com). Edgware Road tube. Lunch served noon-2.30pm, dinner served 6-10.30pm Mon-Sat. Main courses £5.30-£8.50. Set lunch £4.50 1 course, £6.50 3 courses.

7 Hala

Hala may be a simple Turkish eat-in or takeaway joint, but it has always been smart. Waiting staff wear black waistcoats and yellow ties, while the ladies sitting in the window hand-rolling gözleme (filled crêpes) sport matching white T-shirts and hair nets. A revamp has reinvigorated the place a little, but the food and the welcome remain blessedly unchanged. Everything has visual pzazz. Excellent mixed meze makes a colourful feast: houmous, tarama, butter-rich cacık (cucumber with garlic in yoghurt), aubergine salad (patlıcan salatası), cubes of fresh white cheese and ezme (tomato salad). The three 'daily dishes' – stews and pasta – can be served as a mix, but the grill is the main attraction. Succulent lamb with puréed aubergine (alinazik) is a favourite, as are mixed kebab platters on huge plates, and there are a couple of grilled fish options too. *29 Grand Parade, Green Lanes, N4 1LG (8802 4883, www.hala restaurant.com). Manor House tube then bus 29. Meals served 7am-1.30am daily. Main courses £7-£12.*

8 Needoo Grill

Just round the corner from the perennially heaving, crowd-pleasing Tayyabs, and far from a million miles away in concept, Needoo Grill opened in 2009 and continues to be a more civilised provider of Punjabi grills, curries and snacks. The relative lack of queues also means it's a useful and speedy spot for takeaway. Over repeated visits, we've found the food consistently agreeable and the staff friendly, even if the menu does little to differentiate itself from its local counterpart – the restaurant was opened by a former Tayyabs manager. What you get is meaty grills (mutton kebab, lamb chops, king prawns), a few street-food staples (samosa, pakora, paneer tikka roll) and stridently spiced curries ('daighi' dry lamb, dahls, karahi meat dishes). Everything is good value, and there's no corkage on BYO.

87 New Road, E1 1HH (7247 0648, www.needoogrill.co.uk). Aldgate East or Whitechapel tube. Meals served 11.30am-11.30pm daily. Main courses £5-£11.50.

9 Rosa's

The name is coincidental (it belonged to the caff previously occupying the restaurant's original Spitalfields site), but it seems appropriate for this cheery, low-key endeavour, run by an English husband/Thai wife team. The interior is all pale plywood furniture and corrugated-effect panelling, apart from some bright red stools and lampshades. The basement has slightly bigger tables. It's not a comfortable venue; the emphasis is firmly on speedy, budget dining. The lengthy menu covers all the standards – fish cakes, spicy-sour soups, salads, stir fries and curries – with dishes marked with one, two or three chillies to indicate heat. Portions are generous, so you could cut costs by sharing a starter: 'fresh' summer rolls (similar to Vietnamese rice-paper rolls) arrived as four hefty pieces. Green vegetable curry included proper Thai aubergines and big chunks of tofu; som tam (shredded papaya salad with prawns, long beans, cherry tomatoes, cashew nuts and copious lime) is eye-wateringly hot. To drink, there's an assortment of teas (hot and cold), Chang beer and wine.

48 Dean Street, W1D 8BF (7494 1638, www.rosaslondon.com). Leicester Square or Tottenham Court Road tube. Meals served noon-10.30pm Mon-Fri; noon-11pm Sat; 1-10pm Sun. Main courses £7.99-£15.99.

Kitchen Times

Tues-Fri 6pm - 10.30pm
Sat 10am - 2.45pm & 6pm - 10.30pm
Sun 10am - 2.45pm & 6pm -   9.30pm

Last Orders 15 minutes
before kitchen closes

ORFORD SALOON
TAPAS BAR
32 Orford Road, Walthamstow Village E17 9NJ
Tel: 020 8503 6542

Family run bar serving authentic tapas freshly prepared by our Spanish chef
using only the highest quality ingredients.

Sample our exciting selection of Spanish wines, beers and sherries.

All day breakfasts now available from 10am on the weekend.

We are the first tapas bar in London to serve Rioja
beer for both fish and meat.

10 Orchard

This homely café is a cheaper and more casual spin-off from smart vegetarian restaurant Vanilla Black. The retro-style interior has appeal, with its vintage recipe cards pinned to the walls and mismatched crockery. Wicker baskets full of vegetables are displayed in the window, and a counter near the entrance is piled with the day's sandwiches, salads and cakes. It's a pleasant surprise to find an excellent vegetarian café drawing on British ingredients and traditions with such delicious results: russet apple tart with butterscotch sauce, say, or savoy cabbage 'pudding' with a cheddar-laced centre (a main served with a slick of creamed celeriac and a red wine reduction). Golden syrup pudding is a neat tower, garnished with blobs of 'burnt' satsuma and cinnamon-tinged whipped cream. Typical of the 'mug of soup with a sarnie' combo is leek and potato soup with freshly fried croûtons and chive oil garnish, plus wholemeal bread filled with sharp cheddar, chunky chutney and crisp baby beetroot leaves. Note that bookings and credit cards are not accepted.

11 Sicilian Avenue, WC1A 2QH (7831 2715, www. orchard-kitchen.co.uk). Holborn tube. Meals served 8am-8pm Mon-Fri; 10am-7pm Sat. Main courses £6-£7.

11 Meza

This Lebanese restaurant is so popular – and tiny, with room for only 15 customers – that you'll need to book well in advance. Excellent hot and cold meze dishes include houmous, fatayer pastries packed with spinach and onion, stuffed vine leaves, makdous (pickled aubergine filled with walnut) and kibbeh (crisp bulgar wheat shells holding moist minced lamb). Superb grilled mains include shish taouk: cubed chicken and veg on a skewer, cooked to juicy perfection and served the proper way, with an dollop of garlic cream. Drinks include affordable Lebanese wine, and beer from Lebanese Brew, one of the Arab world's newest microbreweries. The setting is nondescript and the service slightly rushed, but the superb food makes Meza a gem. Cash only.

34 Trinity Road, SW17 7RE (07722 111299). Tooting Bec tube. Dinner served 5-11pm Mon. Meals served noon-11pm Tue-Sun. Main courses £8.50-£9.50. Set meze £16.

12 Tsuru

This small Japanese restaurant in the shiny shopping mall behind Tate Modern is aimed at the takeaway crowd with its display case of ready-prepared sushi and salad boxes, and fridge full of canned drinks. You can eat in – perched on leather-topped stools at high shared tables, or at one of the standard tables near the door – but it can get uncomfortably cramped at lunch. Quality is higher than in many high-street sushi outlets, with all food freshly prepared on the premises. Staff are bright and efficient. Katsu curry is the signature dish, the mildly spiced sauce

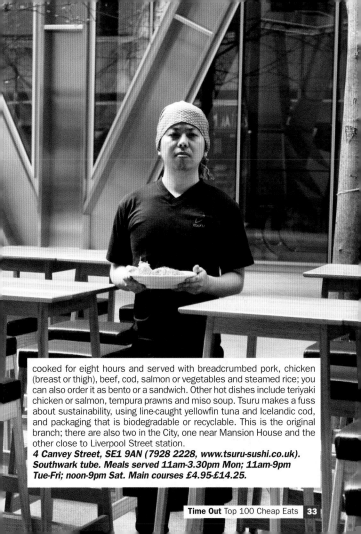

cooked for eight hours and served with breadcrumbed pork, chicken (breast or thigh), beef, cod, salmon or vegetables and steamed rice; you can also order it as bento or a sandwich. Other hot dishes include teriyaki chicken or salmon, tempura prawns and miso soup. Tsuru makes a fuss about sustainability, using line-caught yellowfin tuna and Icelandic cod, and packaging that is biodegradable or recyclable. This is the original branch; there are also two in the City, one near Mansion House and the other close to Liverpool Street station.

4 Canvey Street, SE1 9AN (7928 2228, www.tsuru-sushi.co.uk). Southwark tube. Meals served 11am-3.30pm Mon; 11am-9pm Tue-Fri; noon-9pm Sat. Main courses £4.95-£14.25.

13 Haberdashery

Haberdashery is a brilliant example of the 'make-do-and-mend' café, not just in its aesthetic of vintage crockery, cocktails in jam jars, and hand-written labels, but also in its multifunctional appeal. It also sells books (lovely novellas by local press Peirene) and prints, tea sets, groceries and old-fashioned sweeties, as well as hosting sales, launches and monthly themed supper clubs. Given the (well-handled) weekend waits for one of the tightly packed tables, the tucker has to be good – and it is. From a stunning window display of cakes to the handspan-sized bowls of glossy hot chocolate, this is a professional affair. Brunch might involve a veggie breakfast – nicely fried egg, soft rather than crunchy hash brown, halloumi, a big moist mushroom and excellent greens – or french toast with maple syrup and cinnamon bananas. For lunch, there are the likes of falafel burger or Scandinavian meatballs with Danish cucumber salad and teacup soup. Weekdays are quieter, while in summer trestle tables in the gravel backyard provide more space.

22 Middle Lane, N8 8PL (8342 8098, www.the-haberdashery.com).
Finsbury Park tube/rail then bus W3 or W7, or Crouch Hill rail.
Meals served 8am-4.30pm Mon-Fri; 9am-5.30pm Sat, Sun. Main
courses £5.95-£11.95.

BIG APPLE
Hot Dogs

OUR DOGS DON'T BITE!

HOT DOG CARTS - POP-UPS - MAIL ORDER - PARTIES

"THE DOGS ARE THE BEST IN BRITAIN – NO QUESTION"
GILES COREN – THE TIMES

WWW.BIGAPPLEHOTDOGS.COM
TWITTER.COM/BIGAPPLEHOTDOGS

BITE ME!

14 Gujarati Rasoi

Mother and son Lalita Patel and Urvesh Parvais have been operating as street vendors for a few years, selling the vegetarian dishes of western India at various food markets. Now they have a bricks-and-mortar venture, which, despite impressive food, is something of a work in progress. The dining room is tiny, noisy and minimal. Dishes are partially cooked in their commercial kitchen unit elsewhere and finished off in the restaurant, resulting in some being slightly over- or undercooked. 'Mains' comprising rice, vegetables, dahl or kadhi (a yoghurt 'soup') are piled atop one another, home-style, making individual flavours indiscernible. Oh, but the food. The short, regularly changing menu might include savoury lentil cake 'ohndhwo', gherkin-like baby gourd 'tindora', and 'patra': spirals of colocasia (taro) leaves stuffed with spicy chickpea flour batter. Everything tastes sprightly and vibrant; and the chefs' skill and enthusiasm shines through. The balance of savoury, sweet and tangy flavours is perfect, and the spicing spot-on. The friendly venue takes no bookings, and is currently open only for dinner from Thursday to Saturday. With tweaks this could become a fine Gujarati restaurant.

10C Bradbury Street, N16 8JN (8616 7914, www.gujarati rasoi.com). Dalston Kingsland rail. Dinner served 6-10.30pm Thur-Sat. Main courses £12-£13.

15 Malletti Pizza

The bright yellow signage means Malletti is hard to miss – which is good, because you shouldn't. This little takeaway joint supplies pizza the Italian way: by the rectangular slice, wrapped in paper for munching on the go. Arrayed in colourful strips along the bar, the pizzas on display are an appetising sight. Spicy salami and chilli has a firm, light base, with a rich, sweet tomato topping and a real kick. Crisped courgette and parmesan is brightly herbed with oregano, while potato and sausage is saved from blandness by a generous sprinkling of aromatic rosemary. Malletti also offers a pasta and risotto 'of the day' – perhaps aubergine ravioli in tomato sauce, spicy sausage penne or mushroom risotto. Prices (from £3.95 for a generous slice of pizza, £5.45 for pasta) are good value. There are stools to perch on, but Malletti isn't intended as a sit-in venue. Instead, wander off around Soho, letting the taste of Italy transport you to sunnier climes.

26 Noel Street, W1F 8GY (7439 4096, www.pizzeriamalletti.co.uk). Oxford Circus tube. Meals served 11am-4.30pm Mon-Fri. Dishes £3.95-£5.45.

16 Big Apple Hot Dogs

A mobile cart on Old Street serving specially commissioned sausages made from free-range pork, and buns baked by Anderson's bakery of Hoxton. There are various sizes and meat combinations (pork, beef, pork and beef), and the full range of expected condiments,which are guaranteed to be decorating your top before the last bite. The taste is a revelation for those who would normally avoid hot dogs – coarsely meaty, flavoursome and evocative of baseball games, worlds fairs and competitive eating. Delicious. Check the website for news of a second cart operating at Islington's Chapel Market (Fri-Sun).

In front of 239 Old Street, EC1V 9EY (07989 387441, www.big applehotdogs.com). Old Street tube/rail. Open noon-3pm (winter), noon-6pm (summer) Tue-Fri. Hot dogs £3-£5.

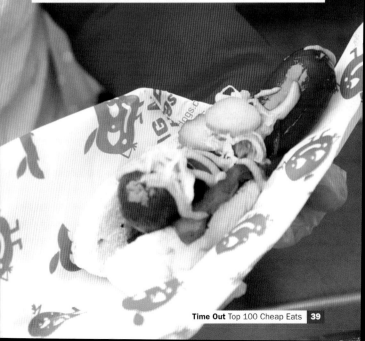

17 Exmouth Market

There aren't many places where you can get a generous helping of hot, delicious food for just £5 – but Exmouth Market on the borders of Clerkenwell and Islington is one such spot. During the week (usually 11.30am-3pm Mon-Fri), ten or so stalls line the street selling a variety of fare, at low prices: from mushroom risotto with rocket salad to falafel wraps with houmous. Thursdays and Fridays are the busiest days.

A few of the street's permanent restaurants set up their own stalls. For example, Spanish/North African star **Moro** (7833 8336, www.moro. co.uk, near right) offers one dish a day – perhaps Moroccan pulled lamb served on flatbread with houmous, salad, a dollop of yogurt and a sprinkle of chilli. On other days, expect pork or chicken variations.

Food vans also appear daily. For tasty vegetarian Indian home cooking, there's the mother-and-son team at **Gujarati Rasoi** (see p37), while **Spinach & Agushi** (7473 5666, www.spinachandagushi.co.uk) provides traditional Ghanaian dishes, such as peanut butter chicken or spinach, ground melon seed (agushi) and mushroom curry.

For decent Thai standards, such as a rich, creamy, authentic-tasting panang curry with a nice amount of spice, look no further than **Simply Thai** (07876 565650). **Spanish Flavours** serves the likes of meatball and potato stew, chickpea and chorizo stew or marinated chicken, all with saffron rice. Other options include Mexican burritos and tacos from **Freebird Burritos** (see p66), hot dogs from **German BBQ** (07889 205786) and vegetarian curries and salads from **Seed** (above right).

Dominique at **Crêpes & Galettes** (below) proffers traditional buckwheat galettes in versions both sweet (Grand Marnier and banana, for example) and savoury (cheese, ham, mushroom and spinach in various combinations); note that he's usually only around on Fridays in summer. And a mouth-watering display of delicious cakes tempts at the **Ion Pâtisserie** stall (@ionpatisserie), including apple strudel, banoffee pie and cheesecake in multiple flavours. *Exmouth Market, between Farringdon Road & Rosoman Street, EC1R 4QL.*

Time Out

AMSTERDAM
Eat | Drink | Shop | Sleep | Explore | Enjoy

BUENOS AIRES
Eat | Drink | Shop | Sleep | Explore | Enjoy

LOS ANGELES
Eat | Drink | Shop | Sleep | Explore | Enjoy

EXPLORE FROM THE INSIDE OUT

Time Out Guides written by local experts

Our city guides are written from a unique insiders' perspective by teams of
local writers covering all you need to know about life in the world's greatest cities

visit timeout.com/store

18 Taqueria

Mexican food is on the ascendancy in London, and this cheerful café serving hearty, classic (if rather workaday) dishes, is among the city's best. The use of authentic ingredients is the key; Taqueria is owned by the same folk as Cool Chile, the Borough Market stalwarts who sell an impressive range of chillies, beans and tortillas (all available in the restaurant's kiosk). Mexican comfort food is its métier. Tortilla soup, with a tomato-chicken stock, is rich and attractively decorated with crisply fried tortillas. You'll find a varied choice among the 15 meat, vegetarian and fish tacos on the menu, and anything with the house-made chorizo is delicious. Drinks run from tequila, margaritas or beer to fresh juices such as watermelon. Leave space for dessert: churros con cajeta – doughnuts that you dip in rich chocolate sauce – are divine. The café's location on Westbourne Grove means that diners are frequently more smartly attired than the casual but pleasant dining room, where old Mexican film posters provide the decoration. Note that bookings are not accepted from Friday to Sunday.

139-143 Westbourne Grove, W11 2RS (7229 4734, www.taqueria. co.uk). Notting Hill Gate tube. Meals served noon-11pm Mon-Thur; noon-11.30pm Fri, Sat; noon-10.30pm Sun. Dishes £3.90-£8.75.

19 Young Cheng

Not to be confused with its bargain-basement siblings on Wardour Street and Shaftesbury Avenue (specialising in buffet dining and one-bowl dishes respectively), this branch of the Young Cheng mini-group is, by Chinatown standards, a smart, sit-down affair. Sure, there are roast ducks dangling in the window, but there are also proper tablecloths, dark glossy furniture and pretty red lanterns. Efficient, welcoming staff serve a wide array of Cantonese fare, but it's the simplest dishes – bowls of steaming noodles for around £5.50 – that remain the most popular. The daily dim sum is also a draw, especially as prices are resolutely low, with most dishes costing under £3. Cooking can lack finesse, but look out for the moist, sticky 'glutinous rice parcel' with its generous, meaty filling (a chunk of Chinese sausage here, a morsel of chicken or shrimp there). Also worth ordering are the sui mai (a classic dumpling quartet, here made with finely minced pork and crab meat) and the shimmering steamed dumplings, densely packed with sweet prawns, chopped chives and tiny diced water chestnuts.

22 Lisle Street, WC2H 7BA (7287 3045). Leicester Square tube.
Meals served noon-11.30pm Mon-Sat; noon-10.30pm Sun.
Main courses £5-£10.

20 River Café

No, not *that* River Café. This particular River Café, opposite the entrance to Putney Bridge tube station, is a fine example of that endangered species, the old-fashioned British caff. The focus of the breakfast menu, predictably, is a mix-and-match full English – generously portioned, and very reasonably priced at £3-£5. Lunch is anchored by hearty British classics, including shepherd's pie, ham, egg and chips, and liver and bacon, all for £5-£6. If you can possibly squeeze in more, apple pie and some tasty Italian puds await. The real draw, however, is not the food, but the feeling of being in a living museum. The place has a quietly dignified, low-key charm, and the decor – unchanged in decades – is a delight, with beautiful blue and white tiling, seascape murals, plywood panelling and Formica tabletops. Italian proprietor Rob offers a warm welcome to all, from elderly gents parked with the newspaper to the few young hipsters who have discovered this gem. Forget the current retro-revival trend; nothing is as comforting as the real thing – ideally with a bacon and egg butty and a cuppa (two sugars, please).

Station Approach, SW6 3UH (7736 6296). Putney Bridge tube.
Meals served 7am-3.30pm Mon-Fri; 10am-3pm Sat. Main courses
£4-£7.

21 Borough Market

If you're happy eating on the hoof, Borough Market is one of the best places in London to find a lunch for around a fiver. Occupying an impressive Victorian glass-vaulted space beneath the arches of a railway viaduct, a few minutes' walk from London Bridge station, this historic food fair is a lively and atmospheric place.

There's always a queue for the chorizo sandwich (rich, spicy sausage, bitter rocket and sweet-sour piquillo peppers, held together in a lightly toasted white roll, £3.75) from Spanish deli **Brindisa** (7407 1036, www.brindisa.com – pictured right). Other meaty options include the shredded duck confit sandwich bursting from a soft white bun (£5), from **Le Marché du Quartier** (7378 8679), and salt beef (cured on-site) served in sturdy ciabatta with pickle and mustard (£6) from **Northfield Farm** (www.northfieldfarm.com).

Bermondsey-based dairy and cheese-maker **Kappacasein** (www.kappacasein.com) has also caused a stir with its toasted cheese sandwich (£5), a humble snack honed to perfection. The combination of montgomery cheddar with leek, onion and garlic between two slices of sourdough bread is so loved that it has its own Facebook fan-page. Enjoy it with a steaming cup of dry cider (£2.50) from **New Forest Cider** (www.newforestcider.co.uk).

The **Total Organics** kitchen has a counter laden with aromatic vegetable dishes; a slice of omelette or tart, plus three salads (ratatouille, chickpea tagine, and rosemary and sweet potato are possible options) costs £5. A falafel wrap (£4) from **Arabica Food & Spice** (www.arabicafoodandspice.com) comes generously portioned with all the trimmings. Try some of their tooth-achingly sweet baklava for afters. Alternatively, pick up some cheese or cured meats from any of the food stalls, along with a loaf of bread from artisan bakery **Flour Station** (www.theflourstation.com), and escape the crowds for an impromptu picnic by the river.

The market exists in skeleton form from Monday to Wednesday, so pop along in the latter half of the week for the full experience. If you want to miss the crowds, a morning visit is advisable.

Borough Market, 8 Southwark Street, SE1 1TL (7407 1002, www.boroughmarket.org.uk). London Bridge tube/rail. Open for lunch 10am-3pm Mon-Wed. Full market 11am-5pm Thur; noon-6pm Fri; 8am-5pm Sat.

▶ *At weekends (9am-2pm Sat, 11am-4pm Sun) the stalls and railway arches around Maltby Street offer more gourmet treats.*

22 | Warung Bumbu

Take a neighbourhood Japanese restaurant, change the signage, hire a Balinese chef, and – faster than you can say rijsttafel – Battersea has a new Indonesian restaurant. The long black tables, shared bench seating and lack of coat hooks mean this isn't the cosiest of places to eat, but the cooking is decent. Our best dish was ikan balado: the fish (ikan) crisp and freshly fried, the stir-fried chilli paste (balado) not so pungent that it annihilated the delicacy of the white fish. Beef rendang was slow-cooked to tenderness, and correctly dry and dark, though the spicing was very timid by Indonesian standards (Warung Bumbu roughly translates as 'spice shack'). Acar kuning – a Balinese vegetable pickle – was an exemplary version, the matchsticks of colourful veg lightly vinegared and a good palliative to sambal belacan, a spicy chilli and shrimp-paste relish. With so few reliable Indonesian restaurants in London, one more place that showcases the cooking is always welcome – just don't expect a re-creation of your holiday in Ubud.

196 Lavender Hill, SW11 1JA (7924 1155, www.warungbumbu. co.uk). Clapham Junction rail. Lunch served noon-3pm, dinner served 6-11pm daily. Main courses £6.99-£9.99.

23 | Piebury Corner

The name is excusable (just) when you find out that this spruce white-tiled corner pie 'deli' is a Gooner operation through and through. It's the offspring of a pie café that pops up in a private home near the old Highbury Stadium (and the new Emirates) on match days, and the pies are named after a hall of fame of Arsenal players. The proprietors no longer have time to do their own baking, so the pies are made off the premises (but to the original recipes) – and they're still delicious. The Charlie George is a proper water-crust Scotch pie; the Ray Parlour encases pork, apple and stuffing in a thin layer of golden pastry; the Tony Adams is a meat-packed steak and ale, and the Viera'getarian melts cheese with potato and garlic. Most pies cost £6.50 (except the fancy-pants Thierry Henry venison) to eat in with mash or roasties and gravy. You can get dessert pies too, and bottled ale.

209-211 Holloway Road, N7 8DL (7700 5441, www.pieburycorner. com). Highbury Corner tube/rail. Open 11am-7pm Tue-Thur; 11am-5pm Fri, Sat; and Arsenal match days. Pies £4.50-£7.

24 Baozi Inn

This Chinatown café is a great drop-in spot for Beijing and Chengdu-style street snacks. The decor, inspired by Beijing's hutongs (alleys) circa 1952, signals Communist Revolution kitsch. The scale of the interior is also authentically mid-20th-century Chinese in that the wooden seats and tables are best suited to diners of smaller stature. True to Sichuanese form, red is present in most dishes – as a slick of potent chilli oil, or in lashings of sliced or whole chillies. This is a good place to try a big bowl of dan dan noodles, with their mild heat and the slightly numbing effect of Sichuan pepper in the ground pork sauce (the dish was over-salted on our most recent visit). The dumplings in soup are also a good choice. The eponymous baozi is a steamed roll filled with pork or vegetables, a dish typical of northern China. These can also be bought at the tiny takeaway shop next door, where a huge pot of chillies and Sichuan pepper boils like a witches' cauldron. This is used as the hotpot for assorted skewers (lamb, cuttlefish ball, shiitake mushroom, dried bean curd, hollow 'prawn balls'), which cost a mere £1-£1.20 each and cook in around two minutes.

26 Newport Court, WC2H 7JS (7287 6877). Leicester Square tube. Meals served 11am-10pm daily. Main courses £6.50-£7.50.

25 Rasa

The original branch of the Rasa chain is still going strong, serving the vegetarian dishes from Kerala with which it broke the anglicised curry-house mould in 1997. The hot-pink interior sees a roaring weekend trade, thanks to the great Indian cooking at very reasonable prices. Following snacks (not just poppadoms, but achappam and pappadavadai too) with pickles, you could have a masala dosa, but that hardly seems the point. Instead, get stuck into the more unusual dishes, such as the wonderful moru kachiathu – a turmeric-infused, sweet-sour runny yoghurt dish made with mango and green banana – or a simple rasa kayi: mixed veg in a full-flavoured gravy. Both cost under a fiver. Tamarind rice was under-spiced, but the breads are great – a nice coil of paratha, for instance – and the enticingly dry black-eye bean dish, stir-fried with onions and spices, is a subtle delight.

55 Stoke Newington Church Street, N16 0AR (7249 0344, www.rasarestaurants.com). Stoke Newington rail or bus 73, 393, 476. Lunch served noon-2.30pm Sat, Sun. Dinner served 6-10.30pm Mon-Fri; 6-11.30pm Sat, Sun. Main courses £4-£6.50.

26 Wild Food Café

This café perched above Neal's Yard focuses on serving 'raw' food. Diners sit around the open kitchen, watching chefs employ futuristic techniques to create raw sandwiches, raw desserts and even a daily-changing soup (warmed to no more than 40°C and served at body temperature). A raw 'red thai curry' is also served at room temperature with either raw 'ryce' (tiny chopped veg), or

the real, conventionally cooked stuff. There is plenty more for non-raw diners too, from 'steaming hot' options such as provençal stew to toasted sourdough sandwiches. Sandwich fillings are equally raw and intriguing, from pistachio falafel to raw squash and hemp houmous or coconut and almond 'cheeze'.

1st floor, 14 Neal's Yard, WC2H 9DP (7419 2014, www.wildfood cafe.com). Covent Garden tube. Meals served noon-4.30pm Mon-Wed, Sun; noon-9.30pm Thur-Sat. Main courses £4.80-£12.50.

27 Arancini Factory

Sicily's fried risotto balls (gluten-free here) are the mainstay of this retro-chic caff, a factory outlet for the market stall and event-catering team known as Arancini Brothers. The open kitchen at the back, surrounded by boxes of market-fresh produce, offers just two varieties of the little brown nuggets – original (vegetarian), and mushroom and zucchini (vegan) – but many ways in which to enjoy them. Wrapped in a tortilla with slow-roasted chicken or bacon, perhaps. Or with a hot stew of meat, or aubergine and peppers; or on a salad; or by the handful. Want something else? There's an enticing display of filled bagels, sandwiches and baked goods (cheddar and leek or apple and cinnamon muffins) by the window. Quality coffees at keen prices keep customers rolling in. There's outdoor seating at the rear. No credit cards.

115 Kentish Town Road, NW1 8PB (3648 7941, www.arancini brothers.com). Kentish Town tube/rail. Meals served 8am-4pm Mon-Fri; 9.30am-4pm Sat, Sun. Main courses £4-£7.95.

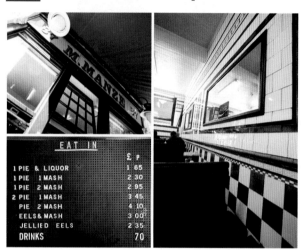

EAT IN	£ P
1 PIE & LIQUOR	1 65
1 PIE 1 MASH	2 30
1 PIE 2 MASH	2 95
2 PIE 1 MASH	3 45
PIE 2 MASH	4 10
EELS & MASH	3 00
JELLIED EELS	2 35
DRINKS	70

London's time-honoured caterers to the workers, pie and mash shops provide food that has altered little since the shops appeared in the middle of the 19th century: potatoes (a wedge of glutinous mash), pies (minced beef and gravy in an impervious crust), eels (jellied and cold or warm and stewed) and a ladleful of liquor (an unfathomable lubricant loosely based on parsley sauce). Escalating eel prices have meant many places only serve pie and mash these days. Vinegar and pepper are the preferred condiments, a fork and spoon the tools of choice. Expect to order in multiples: one pie, two mash; two pies, three mash…

A choice bunch of these establishments remains, many resplendent with tiled interiors, marble-topped tables and worn wooden benches. The oldest and most beautiful is M Manze on Tower Bridge Road, established in 1902, though F Cooke of Broadway Market, the two Kellys and Harrington's all date from the early 20th century. Visit these family-run businesses while you can, for each year another one closes, and with it vanishes a slice of old London. Relish the food, the surroundings and the prices – you'll rarely pay more than a fiver.

WJ Arment, 7 & 9 Westmoreland Road, SE17 2AX (7703 4974).
Castle's, 229 Royal College Street, NW1 9LT (7485 2196).
Clark's, 46 Exmouth Market, EC1R 4QE (7837 1974).
Cockneys Pie & Mash, 314 Portobello Road, W10 5RU (8960 9409).
F Cooke, 9 Broadway Market, E8 4PH (7254 6458).
F Cooke, 150 Hoxton Street, N1 6SH (7729 7718).
AJ Goddard, 203 Deptford High Street, SE8 3NT (8692 3601).
Harrington's, 3 Selkirk Road, SW17 0ER (8672 1877).
G Kelly, 414 Bethnal Green Road, E2 0DJ (7739 3603).
S&R Kelly, 284 Bethnal Green Road, E2 0AG (7739 8676).
AA Manzes, 204 Deptford High Street, SE8 3PR (8692 2375).
L Manze, 76 Walthamstow High Street, E17 7LD (8520 2855).
L Manze, 74 Chapel Market, N1 9ER (7837 5270).
M Manze, 87 Tower Bridge Road, SE1 4TW (7407 2985,
www.manze.co.uk).
M Manze, 105 High Street, SE15 5RS (7277 6181,
www.manze.co.uk).

29 Gambardella

Behind the counter, a Napoli FC pennant hangs alongside a Charlton Athletic one, which just about sums up this unpretentious caff's standing in the neighbourhood. The original 1930s decor sends traditionalists into raptures: the front space is bright with polished, peachy Vitrolite panelling edged with chrome, while the tables and moulded plywood revolving chairs date from the 1960s. The menu – fry-ups and Italian specials – is a joy for the impecunious, with toast at 60p and a cappuccino for £1.60. Or you can push the boat out with a soft, toasty panini of chargrilled courgettes, tomatoes and mozzarella. Carb-loading options are plentiful: as well as a full complement of pasta dishes, there are pancakes and baked potatoes with a range of toppings, and comforting fuel such as steak and kidney pudding. Jam roly-poly with custard is £1.60 well spent. Note that it's cash only.

47-48 Vanbrugh Park, SE3 7JQ (8858 0327). Blackheath or Westcombe Park rail or bus 53. Open 8am-4.30pm Mon-Fri; 8am-2pm Sat. Main courses £3-£4.50.

30 Hummus Bros

A laid-back, modern-looking snack bar devoted to the humble chickpea or, more precisely, its creamy offshoot, houmous. What you get is a silky-smooth bowlful, with a dollop of tahini, a sprinkling of paprika and a warm wholemeal pitta, plus a topping of your choice: chunky slow-cooked beef, perhaps, or juicy guacamole with red peppers and red onions, or mashed, cumin-scented fava beans. You can add a side salad – options include zingy tabouleh or barbecued aubergine – or customise your plate with extras such as tortilla chips, carrot sticks or hard-boiled egg. There are also branches in Holborn and on Cheapside. Bookings not accepted.
88 Wardour Street, W1F 0TH (7734 1311, www.hbros.co.uk). Oxford Circus or Tottenham Court Road tube. Meals served noon-10pm Mon-Wed, Sun; noon-11pm Thur-Sat. Main courses £3.70-£8.65.

31 Hai Ha

Things are busy after a spruce-up and the arrival of a new menu at 'the first Vietnamese restaurant on Mare Street': the 'Closed' sign was on display and every table occupied when we tiptoed through the curtained entrance for a pre-booked meal on a Saturday evening. The menu is huge – running from steamed snails, and nicely chargrilled quails served with a fruity onion salad and some fierce chillies, to hot pots and very salty, crunchily battered pieces of sea bass. Many diners will go no further than the classic Vietnamese pho (noodle soup), which comes in half a dozen varieties, served in a big bowl and accompanied by a little dish of bean sprouts, parsley, red chillis and a slice of lemon. Look past the wine list and Saigon beer to try the syrupy-sweet lime juice. Staff were hard-pressed, but cheerful – and attentive with glasses of tap water.

206 Mare Street, E8 3RD (8985 5388, www.haiha.co.uk).
London Fields rail. Meals served noon-11am Mon-Sat.
Main courses £3.60-£7.80.

32 Meat Liquor, Meat Market, Meat Mission

Meat Liquor (pictured), one of 2012's hippest London restaurants, was opened by Yianni Papoutsis after he'd spent a few years driving his Meat Wagon mobile grill around town. Along with his famed burgers, it serves up a serious side order of attitude. Wires dangle from the ceiling, walls are violently graffitied, it's eerily dark and grungy, and the rockabilly/hillbilly/garage is turned up loud. Yianni has clearly done his research into the underrated artform that is the US hamburger: everything, down to the enamel tin it's served on, is pitch-perfect. Patties are 100% beef, topped with additions such as pickles, cheese, red onions, chilli or the secret 'dead hippie' sauce, and served in a glazed bun. Other dishes include sweet and spicy buffalo wings, fried pickles (very Deep South), coleslaw and chilli dogs: kitchen roll is provided to compensate for the lack of cutlery – and you'll need it. It's good value and the closest you'll get to a down 'n' dirty diner without crossing the Atlantic. Next came Meat Market, a brighter but even more fast-paced burger and hot dog joint above Covent Garden Market. No bookings are taken at either place, so expect to queue. Latest addition Meat Mission is similarly dark and grungy, but does accept reservations.

Meat Liquor, 74 Welbeck Street, W1G 0BA (7224 4239, www.meat
liquor.com). Bond Street tube. Meals served noon-11pm Mon-Thur;
noon-1am Fri, Sat; noon-9.30pm Sun. Main courses £6-£8.
Meat Market, The Mezzanine, Jubilee Market Hall, Tavistock
Street, WC2E 8BE (www.themeatmarket.co.uk). Covent Garden
tube. Meals served noon-11pm Mon-Sat; noon-10pm Sun. Main
courses £6-£8.
Meat Mission, 14-15 Hoxton Market, N1 6HG (7739 8212,
www.meatmission.com). Old Street tube/rail. Meals served noon-
midnight Tue-Sat; noon-10pm Sun. Main courses £6-£9.

33 Best burritos

At the **Daddy Donkey** burrito stall (Leather Lane Market, EC1N 7TE, www.daddydonkey.co.uk, open 11am-3pm Mon-Fri, right), the queue is so long you just know there's something good waiting for you. But you won't have to wait too long, thanks to an ultra-efficient production line of burrito-builders. We like the fajita option (£5.95), which instead of black beans  offers the colour and crunch of grilled onions and sautéed peppers – a terrific foil to chunks of juicy shredded pork.

Mini-chain **Chilango** (76 Chancery Lane, WC2A 1AA, www.chilango.co.uk, open 11.30am-9pm Mon-Fri) serves a pork burrito for £6.70. It's proof that pork doesn't have to be pulled: the piggy option here comes chopped into rustic chunks, with deliciously charred fatty edges. The salsa is mild-mannered – for a more fiery hombre, add Chilango hot sauce. **El Burrito** (5 Charlotte Place, W1T 1SF, 7580 5048, open noon-3pm, 6-10pm Mon-Fri, below) teams tender, tangy cochinita (slow-cooked pork) with a super-fresh pico de gallo (tomato, onion and coriander salsa), for £6. Nearby is one of the locations of **Freebird Burritos** (Goodge Place, W1T 4LZ, www.freebirdburritos.com, open 10.30am-9.30pm Mon-Fri). The pork burrito (£5) comes loaded with tender pulled pork, slow-cooked in a tangy, fragrant marinade.

34 Begging Bowl

Begging Bowl's colourful contemporary interior isn't typical of a neighbourhood Thai restaurant – not surprising, as the owners are not Thai. In the kitchen is Jane Alty, who trained under Thai food expert David Thompson. Alty also spent some time working in Bangkok on Thompson's book *Thai Street Food*, which is the theme of the Begging Bowl's menu. Interestingly, two of Thailand's most famous street-food dishes – pad thai and som tam (the spicy green papaya salad from the north-east) – are absent; instead, there is a far more interesting selection of less usual stir-fries, salads, curries and grilled dishes, featuring authentic ingredients. Deep-fried puffed-rice cakes with a minced chicken, pork and peanut dip, for example. Dishes may lack the lively complexity of flavour you'd expect in Thailand, but most customers here will probably appreciate the kitchen using chilli in polite moderation.
168 Bellenden Road, SE15 4BW (7635 2627, www.thebegging bowl.co.uk). Peckham Rye rail. Lunch served noon-2.30pm Thur-Sat. Dinner served 6-10pm Tue-Sat. Main courses £5.75-£14.50.

35 Fleet River Bakery

This café-bakery's focal point is its heavily laden counter of baked delights. Alongside old favourites (moist carrot or chocolate cake), there are more unusual offerings, such as the 'Fleet Jaffa Slice' and caramel and peanut butter shortbread – all perfect with a cup of quality Monmouth coffee. The cafe's tucked-away location has done nothing to inhibit its success, and lunch hour draws a crowd, much of which is from local offices. Sandwiches, quiches and frittatas are also available, and a daily special is offered from midday, when the scene is reminiscent of a school canteen, with customers queueing for staff to spoon a robust portion of steaming stew, bake or pie on to their plates. Such popularity is not without reason: chicken, mushroom and tarragon lasagne (£7) was an unfussy, filling and tasty affair. Decor has a modern-rustic vibe, with reclaimed-door tabletops adding interest to otherwise unremarkable surroundings. If you don't mind the lack of elbow room, this is a great place to grab a decent lunch for under a tenner.

71 Lincoln's Inn Fields, WC2A 3JF (7691 1457, www.fleetriver bakery.com). Holborn tube. Open 7am-7pm Mon-Fri; 8.30am-5pm Sat. Main courses £5-£7.

36 | Stein's

Stein's Bavarian-style 'beer garden' has two outposts next to the river; one in Richmond and one, the newer site, in Kingston. At the latter, the view from the decked terraces overlooking a leafy section of the Thames is as pretty as any in Munich's Englischer Garten. The interior is tricked out in rustic ski-chalet chic, all rough-hewn woods and chintzy carved hearts, while staff wear lederhosen and dirndls (his and hers Bavarian dress). Weisswurst are terrific: two soft, springy sausages of finely minced pork and veal poached in a delicate broth and correctly served with a freshly baked pretzel and süßer senf (sweet mustard). A classic pork schnitzel (beaten, breadcrumbed and fried until golden brown) may have originated in Austria, but here comes with a south German potato salad with a dressing of oil, vinegar and mustard. End the meal with a terrific sweet dumpling filled with poached apricots and topped with buttery breadcrumbs. Traditional steins of helles and dunkles (pale and dark lagers) come courtesy of Munich breweries Paulaner and Hacker-Pschorr, while weissbier (cloudy wheatbeer) is by Erdinger; wines tour Germany, Austria and Italy. Note that bookings are taken only for groups of six people or more.

56 High Street, Kingston, Surrey KT1 1HN (8546 2411, www.stein-s.com). Kingston rail. Meals served 11am-11pm Mon-Sat; 11am-10pm Sun. Main courses £6.90-£16.50.

DELHI GRILL

Toorie Gajjar
Salad
£1.75

DELHI GRILL

Jaahnwali Salad
£1.75

DELHI GRILL

020 7278 810

DELHI GRILL

020 7278 81

37 Delhi Grill

Islington's answer to a truckers' caff in the Punjab, this shabby-chic canteen is renowned for its earthy home-style cooking at prices that don't bite. Even on weekday evenings, the air is thick with smoky spices and the buzzy conversation of young professionals out for a masala fix. Functional seating arrangements and Indian newspapers plastered across the walls are part of the rough-and-ready appeal, and are complementary to the reassuringly short menu of North Indian staples. There's even a guy making breads by the entrance. The tandoori platters are decent, but the curries are better. Rogan josh – slowly simmered lamb cooked with fried onions, ginger and garlic, spiked with aromatic spices and squished tomatoes – is fabulous for its mellow flavour, and is best enjoyed with griddle-cooked chapatis. Vegetarians get a look-in with such gems as gingery black lentil dahl and quick-fried chopped okra.
21 Chapel Market, N1 9EZ (7278 8100, www.delhigrill.com).
Angel tube. Lunch served noon-2.15pm, dinner served 6-10.30pm daily. Main courses £4.95-£8.95.

38 Banh Mi Bay

Most of London's Vietnamese restaurants are clustered around Shoreditch and Hackney, so it's a bonus to find a more centrally located venue in which to load up on pho (rice noodle soup), summer rolls, banh xeo (pancake) and other Viet classics. At lunchtime, many local workers pop in for takeaway banh mi: a crisp baguette stuffed with pickled carrot and daikon, cucumber, coriander and chilli, plus a filling of your choice – perhaps chargrilled beef or prawn, or spicy pork. Pho comes in beef and chicken variants, plus a vegetarian option that's packed with tofu, mushrooms, carrots and daikon; the broth doesn't have the depth of flavour it could, but is a decent enough rendition. For a zingy starter, go for the goi: crisp, shredded vegetables in a chilli-citrus dressing topped with crushed peanuts, with prawns and pork as optional extras. The decor is more country kitchen than oriental café, with soothing pale green walls, scrubbed pine tables, white-painted chairs and mini chandeliers, and the huge windows mean it's light and bright on even the gloomiest winter's day.

4-6 Theobald's Road, WC1X 8PN (7831 4079, www.banhmibay. co.uk). Chancery Lane tube or 19, 38, 243 bus. Lunch served 11.30am-4pm, dinner served 5.30-9.45pm Mon-Fri. Meals served noon-9.45pm Sat. Main courses £6-£7.50.

39 | Galapagos Bistro-Café

At this tiny neighbourhood bistro you can go globe-trotting through the likes of Moroccan lamb tagine, Corsican beef stew or escalope of chicken milanese. Interiors are low-budget but homely, the laminate flooring and faded upholstery spruced up with colourful cushions and ceiling-hung miniature glitter balls, while a mosaic of a turtle gives a nod to the eponymous group of Pacific islands. Dishes invariably hit all the right notes – witness a well-spiced and fragrant curry of chicken, lentils and split peas. Elsewhere, there are café staples, from breakfasts to burgers. Everything is made on the premises, from pastries to the large collection of own-made preserves (whisky marmalade, and spiced courgette and fennel chutney included). Service is charm itself, and the café brings much-needed cheer to a tired street.

169 Battersea High Street, SW11 3JS (8488 4989, www.galapagos foods.co.uk). Clapham Junction rail. Meals served 9.30am-4pm, dinner served 6.30-9.30pm Tue-Sat. Main courses £7.95-£13.50.

40 Chicken Shop

Run by the Soho House group, this rotisserie is in the basement of their NW5 outpost. As you descend the stairs, it's clear you're in hipster heaven – low lighting, pressed tin ceiling, faux-factory fittings. It's like a little bit of Brooklyn, or a Shoreditch speakeasy bar, in Kentish Town. The service is cheery and fast – you might have to queue, though you can expect to be in and out in under an hour. Bookings are not taken. The choices are chicken, more chicken, or a whole chicken. Half a chicken – enough for two people – costs £8, and the roast bird is served

on enamel platters within seconds of ordering. Side dishes include crinkle-cut fries, coleslaw and corn grilled on the cob. Apple pie is brought with a huge jug of cream, and lashings of nostalgia for a time that never was. There's also a small bar, but most people sup while they eat. Camden Pale Ale (brewed just around the corner) is served on draught at £2.50 for a half pint, or there are glasses of wine – 'House', 'Decent' or 'Good' (£4, £5 or £6).

79 Highgate Road, NW5 1TL (3310 2020, www.chickenshop.com). Kentish Town tube/rail. Dinner served 5pm-midnight Mon-Fri. Meals served noon-midnight Sat; noon-5pm Sun. Chicken £4-£14.50.

41 Bincho

At the centre of Bincho's dimly lit universe is the charcoal grill, where chefs ceaselessly prep and turn skewers of yakitori (from chicken breast and wing to liver and oyster) and kushiyaki (red meat, fish and veg). If you're after culinary adventure, go out on a limb with gizzard and ginkgo nuts or explore off-skewer with whole grilled mackerel pike. Uncooked options include a refreshing salad of squid, salmon, mixed leaves and seaweed tossed in a yuzu (citrus) dressing. Brownie points for rapid-response staff and convivial surroundings, including a whisky bar in the basement. There's also a branch on Exmouth Market, EC1.

16 Old Compton Street, W1D 4TL (7287 9111, www.bincho.co.uk).
Leicester Square or Tottenham Court Road tube. Lunch served
noon-3pm Tue-Fri; 12.30-3.30pm Sat; 1.30-3.30pm Sun. Dinner
served 5-11pm Mon-Sat; 5-10.30pm Sun. Dishes £3-£7.50.

42 | Le Rif

It's tough finding a tagine for under a tenner in this town. But at Le Rif, only one dish on the extensive menu costs more than £5. This Finsbury Park eaterie isn't remotely atmospheric, although there's much to be said for a North African restaurant free of Arabic clichés. Instead, it caters to a local lunchtime crowd, many of whom eschew the North African offerings for sandwiches, jacket potatoes and spaghetti bolognese. Of the Moroccan dishes, the starters (a mild lentil, chickpea and rice soup, say, or houmous with olives and flatbread) are less impressive than the mains. With a combination of spinach, olives, potato, aubergine and lemon, the fish tagine got that balance of sweet and savoury flavours absolutely correct. Couscous royale was every bit as successful, with tender, succulent chunks of chicken and lamb in a subtly spicy broth. There's only one way to end a great Moroccan meal – with pastries and a cup of fresh mint tea – although it does feel a little surreal to pour tea from a beautiful brass pot in a Finsbury Park caff. Note that credit cards are not taken, and alcohol is not allowed.

172 Seven Sisters Road, N7 7PX (7263 1891). Finsbury Park tube/rail. Meals served 8am-10pm Mon-Fri; noon-10pm Sat, Sun. Main courses £4-£6.

43 Manchurian Legends

Manchurian Legends, cousin of nearby Leong's Legends, offers faithful renditions of the hearty rib-sticking cuisine from across China's frosty north. Robust stews from the north-east are well executed, with rich and tender meat: braised pork with glass noodles, say, or stewed chicken with tea-tree mushrooms. The true test of a restaurant serving north-western Chinese food is whether it can properly execute yang rou chuan, the classic Muslim lamb kebabs that are popular (and delicious) street food throughout the People's Republic. Small morsels of nicely fatty lamb are cooked until the fat melts, and liberally doused in the signature chilli-cumin-sesame topping – and Manchurian Legends serves the best we've had in London.

16 Lisle Street, WC2H 7BE (7287 6606, www.manchurian legends.com). Leicester Square or Piccadilly Circus tube. Meals served noon-10.30pm Mon-Wed, Sun; noon-11pm Thur-Sat. Main courses £7-£25. Set lunch £5.50-£11. Set dinner £18.80-£23.80.

44 Brixton Market

The covered arcades of Brixton Market have been transformed in the past couple of years. Once shabby, neglected and with too many empty units, Brixton Village Market (formerly Granville Arcade) and Market Row are now home to more than 20 cafés, restaurants and takeaways, and have become Brixton's culinary and cultural hub. The community atmosphere ramps up on Thursday and Friday nights, when the market stays open late and musicians play. Many restaurants open for lunch too, though not every day (Mondays and Tuesdays are particularly quiet), so phone ahead if you're making a special trip. Some serve alcohol, some offer BYO, many take cash only. Premises can be cramped and seating limited, though you'll find tables 'outside' too – covered but chilly in cold weather.

Our pick of the bunch in Brixton Village Market includes café/pizza joint **Agile Rabbit** (Unit 24, 7738 7646), the prime place to grab a seat if you want a commanding view of the bands that perform in the market passageway outside (from around 8.30pm). Opposite is **French & Grace** (Unit 19, http://saladclub.wordpress.com), a tiny outfit with just three tables that offers a selection of Middle Eastern dishes, notably salads and wraps. Next door, family-run **Mama Lan** (Unit 18, http://mamalan.co.uk) specialises in Beijing street food, from pan-fried or boiled dumplings to deep-fried vegetable dough balls and noodle soups. You can watch the dumplings being expertly made by hand; the king prawn and water chestnut version is sensational.

Also family-run, Thai restaurant **KaoSarn** (7095 8922, above) conjures up complex and authentic flavours that you can only dream of finding at Thai outlets charging twice the price elsewhere in London. One of the most popular choices is the grilled half chicken with som tam (spicy papaya salad) and sticky rice. **Okan** (Unit 39, www.okanbrixton village.com) deals in Osaka-style okonomiyaki, an iconic savoury pancake dish, while teeny Pakistani café **Elephant** (Unit 55, 07715 439857, www.elephantcafe.co.uk) serves a very concise menu at very low prices: own-made samosas, curries and three types of thali (minced lamb, chicken or vegetable).

Colombian restaurant **El Rancho de Lalo** (Unit 94) isn't part of the new wave of eateries; it's been around for years and is still packed at lunchtimes. **Brixton Village Grill** (Unit 43, 07894 353561, http://brixton-villagegrill.com) is a Portuguese/British crossover specialising in chargrilled meat and fish, served with rice or chips and the restaurant's own-made spicy piri-piri sauce. For more fishy fare, this time with a Caribbean slant – ackee and saltfish, or seafood curry with rice and peas, say – and a warm welcome, there's **Etta's Seafood** (Unit 85, 7737 1673, www.ettaskitchen.com). ▶

▶ With a kitchen, eating area and shop in different units, **Cornercopia** (07919 542233, http://brixtoncornercopia.ning.com – left) is pricier than some places, but takes its 'local-is-best' ethos very seriously, sourcing ingredients for its seasonal menu (and own-made jams and preserves) from the market itself or the wider south London area. Seasonality is key to the fresh pasta dishes and own-made breads at Italian restaurant **Bellantoni's** (Unit 81, 07872 945675, www.bellantonis.co.uk). Also here is the original – and still very popular – branch of **Honest Burgers** (Unit 12, 7733 7963, see p114).

The other covered arcade is Market Row, where the premises tend to be bigger and lighter, more like conventional restaurants. Here, you'll find acclaimed pizzeria **Franco Manca** (see p142), one of the first of the Brixton new wave, as well as upmarket burger joint **Bukowski Grill** (Unit 10, 7733 4646, www.bukowski-grill.co.uk) and charcuterie specialist/eaterie **Cannon & Cannon** (Unit 18, 7501 9152, www.cannonandcannon.com).

Cocktail bar **Seven at Brixton** (Unit 7, 7998 3309, http://sevenatbrixton.wordpress.com) serves Spanish pintxo and tapas, and **Casa Morita** (Unit 9, 8127 5107, www.casa morita.com) is a popular option for its crowd-pleasing blend of Mexican food and margaritas. **Rosie's** (Unit 14E, 7733 0034, www.rosiesdelicafe.com), a small, charming, vintage-styled deli-café run by cookery writer Rosie Lovell, is one of the older ventures, opened in 2005, while fried-chicken joint **Wishbone** (Unit 12, 7274 0939, www.wishbonebrixton.co.uk – right) is one of the newest, serving pimped-up junk food (chicken nuggets, mac 'n' cheese) and cocktails in a noisy, colourful, self-consciously trendy setting.

Brixton Village Market & Market Row, both accessible from Coldharbour Lane or Atlantic Road, SW9 (http://bmtf.org.uk). Arcades open 8am-6pm Mon-Wed; 8am-midnight Thur-Sat; 8am-5pm Sun. Restaurant times vary.

45 Tbilisi

Tbilisi is a good-value introduction to Georgian cookery (a popular cuisine across the former Soviet bloc, but rare in the UK). Few diners will fail to appreciate khachapuri (soft yeasty flatbread stuffed with cheese) and the intriguingly spiced salads of puréed aubergine, carrot, leeks and beetroot. A mixed plate is ideal for sharing. The kitchen's secret is the Georgian spice-mix of khmeli suneli, and the ubiquitous blend of marigold and crushed walnuts combined with fresh coriander – all good for vegetarians. For meat-eaters, warmly spiced lamb stews such as chanakhi (slow-braised with tomato and aubergine to tender perfection) are often a better bet than chicken dishes. Don't miss the Georgian wine; the great Kindzmarauli and Khvanchkara are something of an acquired taste with their rich, complex semi-sweetness, but there are also fresh whites such as Tsinandali and a lightly fruity Mtatsminda rosé. Like the restaurant itself, they're a refreshingly different experience.
91 Holloway Road, N7 8LT (7607 2536). Highbury & Islington tube/rail. Dinner served 6-11pm daily. Main courses £8.50-£13.

46 Roti Joupa & Roti Stop

Homesick Trinidadians come to Clapham's Roti Joupa for a culinary pick-me-up, whether it's curried goat (with rice or roti), macaroni pie (served hot or cold) or doubles (roti filled with chickpea curry – the ultimate street snack). Choose a roti filling (goat, lamb, chicken, veg or pumpkin) and then the level of chilli heat (mild, medium or hot). There's also buss-up shot (a sort of beaten-up roti) and pholourie (fried dough balls, here served with tamarind sauce). There are a few stools for perching, but this is mainly a takeaway operation, with a small open kitchen (pictured) and a friendly team cooking up a storm. It's all delicious, and prices are keen, with doubles costing just £1.50 and curried goat roti £5.50.

Less stellar, but worth a visit if you're in north-east London, is Roti Stop. This small, basic outlet advertises more items than it actually has at any one time, but you can't really argue with doubles at £2 and ackee and saltfish at £1.50. It's good, filling stuff – roti filled with boneless chicken curry (pepper and tamarind sauces on request) was a generous portion for £5.50. Guinness punch goes down a treat too. You can just about eat-in, but most of its trade is in takeaways; the badly tuned sound system makes lingering inadvisable.

Roti Joupa, 12 Clapham High Street, SW4 7UT (7627 8637).
Open noon-11pm Mon-Sat. Clapham North tube. Dishes £5.50-£6.50.
Roti Stop, 36B Stamford Hill, N16 6XZ (8815 4433).
Open 10am-10pm Mon-Thur; 10am-11pm Fri; 11am-11pm Sat.
Stoke Newington rail. Dishes £5.50.

47 City Càphê

Long before you see this charming little Vietnamese café, you'll smell some enticing aromas wafting down the street. At lunchtime, you can expect to see a line of City workers at the door; staff are calmly efficient, so don't baulk at the length of the queue – it disappears in no time. The menu is easy to follow. Choose from lightly spiced noodle soups (bun hue or pho), Vietnamese baguettes (banh mi), vermicelli salads, jasmine rice dishes and spring rolls. Most options are available with beef, pork, chicken or tofu – and there's a prawn soup. The 'classic pork' banh mi comes with a succulent cold cut of pork, earthy liver pâté, fiery chilli, crunchy veg and fresh coriander, all in a light crispy baguette. Vegetarian rice-paper summer rolls, with a hint of lemongrass, are delicate and refreshing. Seating in the bright, modern interior is limited, so City Càphê is not the place for a long and lingering lunch, but it's perfect for a quick bite or a tasty takeaway.

17A Ironmonger Lane, EC2V 8EY (www.citycaphe.com).
Bank tube/DLR. Meals served 11.30am-4.30pm Mon-Fri.
Dishes £3.75-£6.50.

48 | Café Below

This long-running café in the crypt beneath St Mary-le-Bow Church serves satisfying breakfasts and lunches. Descend the stone stairs and queue at the kitchen counter for hot dishes (lamb burger or salmon fish cakes, perhaps), salads (rice, puy lentil and mushroom) or sandwiches (Porterford sausages and onion marmalade). It's busy for takeaway lunches, but many people eat in – at the crammed wooden tables in the rough-walled crypt itself, or outside in the courtyard. Avoid the 1-2pm slot if you want to be sure of a seat. Cooking is hearty rather than refined, and vegetarians fare well (the café was veggie-only for years) with the likes of courgette and feta filo pie with salad leaves. Puds, such as comforting rhubarb crumble and custard, or a slice of rich, mousse-like chocolate espresso tart, are worth a punt. Oft-replenished jugs of tap water with mint and lemon halves are a welcome touch.

St Mary-le-Bow, Cheapside, EC2V 6AU (7329 0789,
www.cafebelow.co.uk). St Paul's tube or Bank tube/DLR.
Meals served 7.30am-2.30pm Mon-Fri. Main courses £5-£10.

49 Indian YMCA

The concrete and glass postwar building looks institutional, but has become an institution: for 60 years, the Indian YMCA has successfully fed generations of Indian students newly arrived in the UK. Queue canteen-style at the counter, while checking off the low prices on the pegboard menu above; 'tin fruits 75p' is typically succinct. The freshly prepared curries (fish, mutton, veg, chicken) are all cooked home-style and sensitively spiced. The dahl is a comforting version, and mounds of rice soak up the sauces (be warned that the pilau rice uses generous sprinklings of vivid food colouring). Although most dishes are North Indian in style, dahi vada (lentil rissole in yoghurt) is a soothing South Indian breakfast snack. The Y is better for lunch than dinner, when a limited-choice set meal for £7 is the deal.

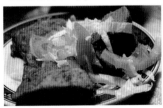

41 Fitzroy Square, W1T 6AQ (7387 0411, www.indianymca.org). Great Portland Street or Warren Street tube. Meals served 7.30-9.15am, noon-2pm, 7-8.30pm Mon-Fri; 8-9.30am, 12.30-1.30pm, 7-8.30pm Sat, Sun. Main courses £2.50-£5.

50 Lombok

Lombok has been producing the same superb South-east Asian staples for years. Friendly, family-run and low-key in design – the small room of wooden tables is still dominated by an old-school dark-wood bar – the place is always packed on Friday and Saturday nights. The menu covers classic dishes from across the region, taking in Burma, Vietnam, Malaysia, Indonesia and Thailand. The Singapore chilli crab is impressive, if messy to eat: a whole crustacean served with an explosion of crispy noodles and a thick, sweet sauce of ginger, onion and spices. Thai green curry is no namby-pamby creamy-coconut dish – it really packs a punch. Padang chicken is a less full-on dish, though it's still a complex compilation of sweet, citrussy and spicy flavours.

17 Half Moon Lane, SE24 9JU (7733 7131). Herne Hill rail or bus 37. Dinner served 6-11pm Mon, Fri, Sat; 6-10.30pm Tue-Thur. Main courses £6-£8.95.

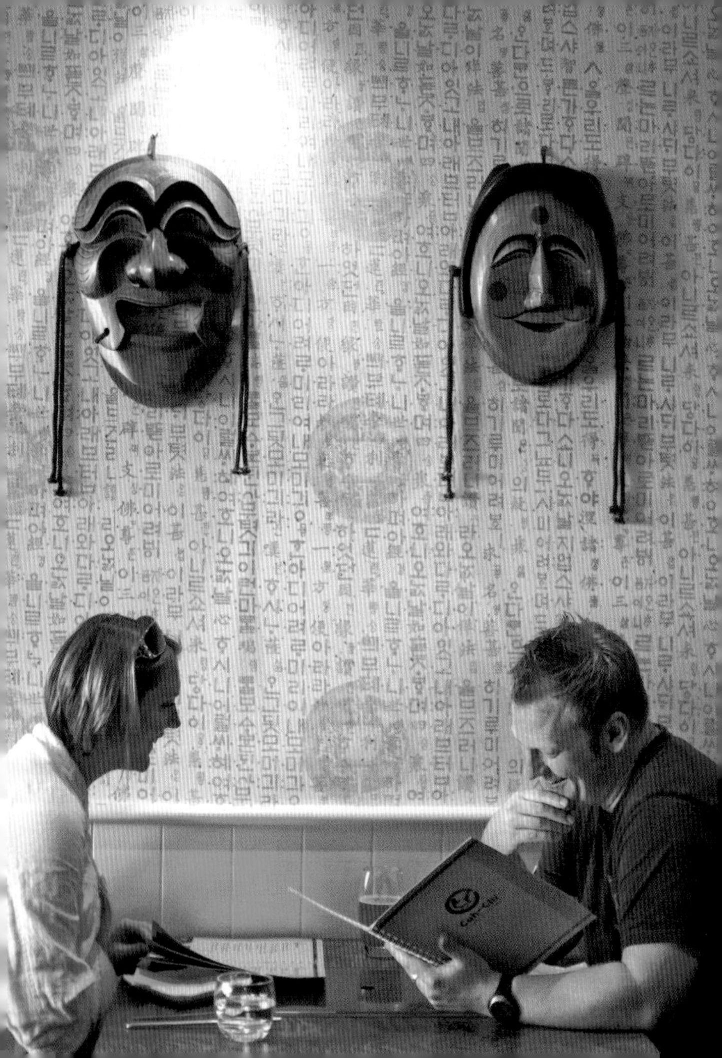

51 Cah Chi

Nearer the centre of London than New Malden's cluster of Korean restaurants, Cah Chi is only minutes away from Raynes Park railway station in a quiet residential street of mock-Tudor frontages, cherry trees and twitching net curtains. Yet the menu makes no concessions to its suburban setting, and is aimed at Korean diners with its barbecue tables and specials list that includes challenging dishes such as raw, fermented skate wing. Non-Korean diners are welcomed too, though, by smiling, English-speaking staff and a menu that has been considerately, though not accurately, translated into English – some pork and chicken dishes have been marked as 'vegetarian'. One of the signature dishes is soondae, a black pudding of sweet potato vermicelli and blood inside a casing of pig chitterlings. Although delicious, the intestinal smell is not to everyone's taste; in this case, order the soondae stir-fried with perilla leaves (called soondae-bokkeum). This dispels the soondae's aroma, and the heat can be adjusted by the addition of spicy chilli paste. The branch in Earlsfield (394 Garratt Lane, SW18 4HP, 8946 8811) has a more mainstream menu, and attracts many non-Korean customers. You can bring your own wine (corkage £2), but not beer.

34 Durham Road, SW20 0TW (8947 1081). Raynes Park rail or 57, 131 bus. Lunch served noon-3pm, dinner served 5-10.30pm Tue-Fri. Meals served noon-10.30pm Sat, Sun. Main courses £6-£14.

52 Afghan Kitchen

Not much changes at this long-running restaurant overlooking Islington Green. The two-floor premises are bright and clean, with spring-green and grey paintwork, simple blond-wood tables and stools, and no decoration beyond a few pot plants. The menu of Afghan home cooking is equally straightforward: eight dishes (three meat, one fish, four vegetarian) of which the focus is hearty warming stews that feature plenty of yoghurt and mint. Spicing is subtle rather than fiery. Moong dall is a comforting, thick, rich purée, while 'Sarah's' combines chickpeas, kidney beans and chunks of potato in a yoghurty sauce. Meltingly soft aubergine and thick slices of orange pumpkin come drizzled in yet more yoghurt. The best method is to come in a group, so you can share dishes – though you can order half-portions to get more variety. Sides include tangy pickles, plain rice and (in the evening) a communal loaf. Fresh-squeezed carrot juice and a few beers and wines are among the drink options, though dogh – watery, mint-inflected yoghurt – is the most refreshing choice. Bring cash as cards aren't taken.

35 Islington Green, N1 8DU (7359 8019). Angel tube. Lunch served noon-3.15pm, dinner served 5.30-10.45pm daily. Main courses £6.50-£7.50.

COFFEES		
	S	D
Espresso	1.35	1.60
Macchiato	1.40	1.70
	M	L
Latte	1.90	2.30
Cappuccino	1.90	2.30
Mocha	1.80	2.40
Frappuccino	2.40	2.70

HOT DRINKS

FRESH MINT TEA sm 1.50 / lge 2.50

TEAS 1.50
Earl grey, peppermint, jasmin, camomile, green, pomegranate

HOT CHOCOLATE 2.20 2.90

FROZEN YOGHURT SMOOTHIES

COLD DRINKS	
Coca cola	1.40
Diet coke	1.40
Mirinda orange	1.40
Perrier water	1.40
Still water	1.40
7 up	1.40

FRESH JUICES

COMBINATION	SOLO
Apple and mint	Apple
Apple and orange	Orange
Carrot and apple	Melon
Carrot and orange	Carrot
Carrot and ginger	
Apple, mint and cucumber	
Apple and melon	

MEZZE

Mezze Pla

Mezze Plat

53 | Comptoir Libanais

A bright, fun Lebanese café, Comptoir Libanais is part canteen, part delicatessen. One wall is lined with shelves containing preserves and other imported goods. The rest of the space is taken up with colourful tables and chairs. Dishes are clearly displayed behind the counter, and there are plenty to choose from: salads, tagines, wraps, and mountains of glistening pastries and baklava. Fruit juices come in a variety of interesting and vitamin-packed flavours, with apple, mint and cucumber a highlight. There are a few branches across town now, in South Kensington, Soho and both Westfield shopping centres.
65 Wigmore Street, W1U 1PZ (7935 1110, www.lecomptoir.co.uk). Bond Street tube. Meals served 8am-10.30pm Mon-Sat; 8am-9.30pm Sun. Main courses £5.85-£12.95.

54 Regency Café

Behind its black-tiled art deco exterior, this classic caff has operated on the quiet Westminster/Pimlico borders since 1946. Customers sit on brown plastic chairs at Formica-topped tables, watched over by muscular boxers and Spurs stars of yore, whose photos hang on the tiled walls. Lasagne, omelettes, salads, baked potatoes, every conceivable cooked breakfast (the chunky bangers are especially fetching) and mugs of tannin-rich tea are meat and drink to the Regency. Stodgetastic own-made specials include steak pie – the thick pastry hiding tender meat in a tomatoey sauce, served with serviceable chips, thick gravy, and peas that might well have seen the inside of a tin. Still hungry? The improbably gigantic cinnamon-flavoured bread and butter pud will see you right for the rest of the week.

17-19 Regency Street, SW1P 4BY (7821 6596). St James's Park tube or Victoria tube/rail. Open 7am-2.30pm Mon-Fri; 7am-noon Sat. Main courses £2.95-£6.50.

55 | Naamyaa Café

This beautifully designed, well-priced restaurant is a blueprint for a new oriental chain (it's a sister brand of Busaba Eathai) – a branch is planned for Shoreditch. Thai food enthusiasts will be thrilled by the menu. The Naamyaa set meals mean you order beef, chicken, prawn or veg, and the kitchen does the rest. Kanom jin – soft, thin rice noodles served at room temperature – are topped with a curry-like sauce of your choice. The side salads might include pickled morning glory, beansprouts, chinese leaves, starfruit and sweet basil to vary the textures and flavours

to your own taste. Not all the dishes are Thai, though. The array of small plates covers Japanese, Malaysian and Chinese dishes; jasmine tea-smoked baby back pork ribs is one of the highlights of the menu. The oddest feature is the smattering of western dishes. Burgers with chips, caesar salad and salad niçoise might be truly international dishes, but they sit uneasily on this pan-oriental menu. Bookings are not taken, so expect to queue at peak times.

Angel Building, 407 St John Street, EC1V 4AB (3122 0988, www.naamyaa.com). Angel tube. Meals served 9am-11.30pm Mon-Sat; 10am-10.30pm Sun. Main courses £7.50-£12.

56 19 Numara Bos Cirrik I

One of many Turkish restaurants lining Stoke Newington Road, 19 Numara is a hardy perennial – it's among the strip's more popular joints, and we've yet to experience a slip in its high standards. There's a good range of traditional starters: the likes of imam bayıldı, patlıcan soslu (aubergines and green peppers in a tomato sauce, served cold) and mücver. You'll also find plenty of dips: ıspanak tarator (puréed spinach and yoghurt), houmous and tarama. Don't order too much, as little plates of salad – onions with pomegranate sauce, finely chopped mixed salad, and another onion salad – come free with main courses. Mains are reliably good: lamb sis is succulent, the full mixed kebab (for two to three) is enormous, and ískender kebabs are generous and flavoursome. The atmosphere is convivial too. Prices have risen over the past few years,

but 19 Numara is still good value and there are now several branches in the area. Alcohol is available, but you can also BYO (corkage costs £1-£5).

34 Stoke Newington Road, N16 7XJ (7249 0400, www.cirrik1. co.uk). Dalston Kingsland rail or 76, 149, 243 bus. Meals served noon-midnight daily. Main courses £7-£13.50.

57 | Pavilion Café

A popular café housed in the domed pavilion on Victoria Park's lake, where the sheer number of outdoor tables means you can usually get a seat, even when it's heaving. An extensive all-day breakfast menu includes three types of eggs benedict, kippers, pancakes, things on toast and variations on a full English. A short lunch list features burgers, a BLT and salads such as beetroot, ricotta, puy lentil and watercress, served with focaccia. Cakes run from chocolate brownie to grapefruit brioche. Staff are well drilled and knowledgeable. All in all, much more than your average park café.

Victoria Park, Crown Gate West, E9 7DE (8980 0030, www.the-pavilion-cafe.com). Mile End tube then bus 277, 425. Meals served 8am-5pm (summer), 8.30am-4pm (winter) daily. Main courses £6.50-£9.

58 Morito

Influences from southern Spain, Turkey and the Levant make for an exciting tapas menu at Morito – little sibling to acclaimed Spanish/North African restaurant Moro next door. The wipe-clean orange surrounds and cramped seating, on stools at the central bar or at small tables, don't make for the most comfortable dining experience. Sitting at the bar means you get to watch the chefs at work on dishes such as crisp, cinnamon-spiced bits of lamb atop creamy aubergine, with chickpea purée and pine nuts –an object lesson in mixing spices and textures. Some small plates don't always justify their price tags, but the ultra-fresh flatbreads and lightly leavened rounds are well worth the £2.50 per basket. There's a short cocktail list, as well as sherries and Spanish wines. No bookings are taken at dinner, though staff will phone you when a table is ready, so you don't have to queue in the cold.

32 Exmouth Market, EC1R 4QE (7278 7007, www.morito.co.uk). Angel tube or Farringdon tube/rail or bus 19, 38, 341. Tapas served noon-4pm, 5-11pm Mon-Sat; noon-4pm Sun. Tapas £1-£8.50.

59 Sedap

The small, family-run Sedap occupies an unassuming spot opposite LSO St Luke's, making it handy for pre- or post-concert dining. Start with archard (a pleasing mix of lightly pickled veg with crushed peanut and sesame seed) rather than the so-so chicken satay. For a main course, it's hard to beat curry tumis (a fish version had sea bream), which arrives in a sturdy copper bowl and exemplifies the typical hot and sour flavours of Nonya cooking (a fusion of Malay and Chinese cuisines). Malaysian expats will find that a glass of warm, sweet teh tarik ('pulled tea') brings back happy memories. Black furniture and olive green walls add a sense of style to proceedings, as do neat touches such as a glass display cabinet showcasing antique tea sets.

102 Old Street, EC1V 9AY (7490 0200, www.sedap.co.uk).
Old Street tube/rail. Lunch served 11.30am-2.15pm Mon-Fri.
Dinner served 6-10.15pm daily. Main courses £6.80-£11.50.

60 Kitfo House

Oriental fire meets the subtler seasonings typical of the Horn of Africa, by way of standard breakfast fry-ups, in this multifunctional Vauxhall café. The split personality is down to the fact that Kitfo House is essentially an Eritrean restaurant that likes to make the most of its Thai chef at lunchtime. The Thai options are cheaper than the African ones: powerfully flavoured kaeng pa (jungle curry), served with a mound of rice, costs just £5.50. The Eritrean version of scrambled eggs, jumbled with green chillies and chopped tomatoes, is a gloriously tasty dish. It can be served with pitta, or, like the rest of the Eritrean specials, with a whole basket of rolled-up injera (spongy and slightly sour: the national bread) that you use as a scoop or plate. Vegetarians can choose delicious messes of spinach, lentils and cottage cheese, while meat eaters are wowed by tender beef stewed in spices – the restaurant's namesake dish. As a grand finale, treat yourself to the Eritrean coffee ceremony: it's a heady and stimulating experience, with incense and popcorn as the trimmings.
49 South Lambeth Road, SW8 1RH (7735 8915). Vauxhall tube/rail. Meals served 8.30am-11.30pm Mon-Fri; 10.30am-11pm Sat, Sun. Main courses £5.50-£7.95.

61 Mamuska!

This Elephant & Castle café is a highly enjoyable place to eat Polish home cooking at low prices. The café is simple but stylish, and there's a sense of humour at work. 'We have a vast wine selection,' says the menu, 'one white, one red and even a rosé' (there's Zywiec and Tyskie beer too). Orders are taken at the counter – cash only – and delivered swiftly to your table. The food is straightforward, and straightforwardly priced: starters £3, puddings the same, and mains £5. Follow satisfying pierogi with richly flavoured pork shoulder gulasz with mash and you may not be able to manage nalesniki (folded pancakes with a sweetened ricotta-like cheese and chocolate sauce).

1st floor, Elephant & Castle Shopping Centre, SE1 6TE (3602 1898, www.mamuska.net). Elephant & Castle tube/rail. Meals served 7am-midnight daily. Main courses £5.

62 Huong-Viet

Set in the premises of a longstanding Vietnamese community centre, Huong-Viet has an intimate, homely feel. When things get busy, the staff can become wayward, some dishes can be average, and noise levels can become deafening, but on the whole the place is lively and fun. Starters such as traditional Vietnamese pancakes, spring rolls and crispy seaweed lead on to a long list of mains, including pork with aubergine and garlic, sizzling prawns with ginger and spring onion, and more unusual barbecue dishes such as prawns wrapped in pork. Rice vermicelli with seafood, lemongrass and chilli is a big bowlful, with plenty of seafood, including scallops, subtle spicing, and mint adding a distinctive edge. Good, honest, flavourful food – and good value too. Cash only.

An Viet House, 12-14 Englefield Road, N1 4LS (7249 0877). Dalston Junction or Haggerston rail, or 67, 149, 236, 242, 243 bus. Lunch served noon-3.30pm, dinner served 5.30-11pm daily. Main courses £6.50-£11.30.

63 Hot Stuff

Twentysomethings, with digs in the locality, love this no-frills venue on snug little Wilcox Road, bringing a hip vibe that's accentuated by the deep purple walls, mosaic framed mirrors, and fairy lights in the windows. The no-corkage BYO policy is a big draw (there's an off-licence next door), but so is the food – freshly prepared in the open kitchen at the rear. There's a brief menu of standard North Indian dishes, as well as daily specials. Expect complimentary popadums with decent chutneys to start. Highlights include sag chicken (bursting with the flavour of spinach) and piping hot chana dahl, but parties of 'leave it to the chef' diners fare best, with a wider variety of dishes conveyed to their tables (such as tandoori chicken wings). Our bill, like theirs, was £15 a head.

19-23 Wilcox Road, SW8 2XA (7720 1480). Vauxhall tube/ rail. Meals served 11am-10pm Mon-Fri; 1-10pm Sat; 4-10pm Sun. Main courses £3-£8.50.

64 Kerb

A street-food revolution is underway in London, thanks to Kerb. This is the snappy new name for eat.st, which began life a few years ago as a small collective of street-food vendors trading in the temporary walkway north of King's Cross station. Since then, the operation has expanded to a much larger community of food stalls and vans, appearing regularly at four locations across the city.

King's Cross Kerb is still the main site, running weekdays (except Mondays). Expect half a dozen stalls, all offering something different – from pizzas and pulled pork to mussels and meringues. The bar is set high for Kerb vendors; to qualify, traders must adhere to exacting standards of 'flavour, personality and kerbside spirit'. **Bhangra Burger** (07859 004628, http://bhangraburger.com) passes the test with flying colours with its masala fish wrap (£6), which features crunchy cabbage, sauces of fresh mint and sweet mango, and a spicy fish marinade.

Meat-heads will love the sticky, pulled-from-the-bone pork provided by the **Rib Man** (www.theribman.co.uk). There's usually a sizeable queue for his wraps, rolls and ribs (from £6) – add a little extra spice with his own-made chilli sauce. Burritos and burgers are standard fare on the street-food scene, schnitzel and knödel less so. But Austrians Franz and Marco are plugging the gap with their **Speck Mobile** (www.speck mobile.com), serving soft pork dumplings, beef goulash, breaded schnitzel and sauerkraut (£5-£6.50).

For dessert, try the sweet bites (£4 for six) offered by **You Doughnut** (@you_doughnut, pictured above). Delightfully crunchy on the outside, light and fluffy in the centre, these mini doughnuts come topped with maple coffee syrup and chopped pistachios.

Stalls change daily. You can run with the Kerb vibe and just turn up, or check the website to see who's trading where and when. Kerb also appears in the City twice a week and in Bloomsbury once a month.

Kerb (www.kerbfood.com). King's Boulevard, N1C 4AH (Tue-Fri). Gherkin, St Mary Axe, EC2 (Thur). CityPoint, Ropemaker Street, EC1 (Fri). UCLU, Malet Place, off Torrington Place, WC1 (last Wed of month). All 11am-2.30pm.

65 Abu Zaad

It may look rather forbidding, the windows on its corner site obscured by black bars, and it may not be a beauty inside either – a reproduction of an Old Damascene street scene dominates the brown walls – but Abu Zaad is a real neighbourhood hangout, popular with everyone from Somalian women and Arab families to young hipsters. Cheap, honest and very good food is the draw, as well as the genuinely friendly service. Meze dishes cost around £3-£4 and might feature sprightly tabouleh; fuul medames served with tahini and tons of lemony olive oil; and plump, generous kibbeh shamieh (the crunchy shell of cracked wheat contrasting with the spicy minced lamb within). Mains are even more of a bargain. In addition to the usual grills there are dishes rarely seen on restaurant menus: molokhia (lamb cooked with molokhia leaves – jew's mallow – to produce a distinctive, slightly sticky stew), for instance, or spiced grilled chicken with frika (fried bulgar). The restaurant is unlicensed and no alcohol is allowed, but the freshly squeezed juices make a splendid accompaniment.

29 Uxbridge Road, W12 8LH (8749 5107, www.abuzaad.co.uk).
Shepherd's Bush Market tube. Meals served 11am-11pm daily.
Main courses £5-£14.

The Vincent Rooms is staffed, front of house and in the kitchen, by young people training at Westminster Catering College, but they are overseen by experienced chefs and maître d's, and they operate in a sophisticated, beautifully appointed venue, with its own entrance away from the student rumpus. Sit at one of the well-spaced, plain wooden tables and look through large picture windows on to Vincent Square, where Westminster School has its playing fields. The daily changing brasserie menu attracts the most custom (there's also a £25 tasting menu in the haute-cuisine Escoffier Restaurant). Kick off, perhaps, with crab and prawn bisque, or a fine wintry salad of medium-rare mallard breast, handsomely presented with toasted oats and nuts, plus rocket and a few berries for zest. Main course might be grilled sea bass fillets, accompanied by creamy risotto, buttered curly kale and a slice of fennel in tempura batter. The well-priced wine list adds allure, but it's the eager-to-please staff that are most refreshing.

Westminster Kingsway College, 76 Vincent Square, SW1P 2PD (7802 8391, www.thevincentrooms.com). St James's Park tube or Victoria tube/rail. Lunch served noon-2pm Mon-Fri. Dinner served 6-9pm occasional evenings. Main courses £8-£12.

67 Wurst Club

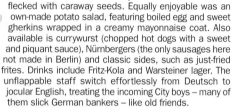

This new fast-food purveyor of the great German sausage is a model of teutonic efficiency and civility. Queue up at the till to place your order, then head to the collection area, where a trio of servers will bag up your just-cooked order. You can eat in, but it won't be comfortable: in traditional German sausage-stand style, there are counters, but no seats.

Cooking is spot-on: the thick, smokey casing of our riesenbockwurst – an extra-long hot dog (riesen means 'giant') – gave way to a juicy pork centre. Instead of a bun, it came with a layer of delicate sauerkraut flecked with caraway seeds. Equally enjoyable was an own-made potato salad, featuring boiled egg and sweet gherkins wrapped in a creamy mayonnaise coat. Also available is currywurst (chopped hot dogs with a sweet and piquant sauce), Nürnbergers (the only sausages here not made in Berlin) and classic sides, such as just-fried frites. Drinks include Fritz-Kola and Warsteiner lager. The unflappable staff switch effortlessly from Deutsch to jocular English, treating the incoming City boys – many of them slick German bankers – like old friends.

56-57 Cornhill, EC3V 3PD (7283 8008, www.the-wurst-club.co.uk). Bank tube. Open 11am-4pm Mon-Fri. Dishes £4-£8.95.

68 | 101 Thai Kitchen

A short walk from Stamford Brook tube, this unassuming family-run restaurant offers relatively inexpensive but fairly authentic food from the north-eastern Thai region of Isarn ('101' is the translation of 'Roi Et', an Isarn province known for the 11 satellite towns around its main city). The region's food is pretty spicy and, in place of fish sauce, uses pla ra (a paste of fermented salted freshwater fish) and plenty of lime juice. The atmosphere of the brightly painted room is inviting and comfortable, staff are pleasant, and tables are reassuringly dotted with South-east Asian diners. Try curried soft-shell crab with celery and spring onions, or fried rice packed with prawns, and nicely suffused with chilli, garlic and holy basil, or one of the many versions of som tam salad.

352 King Street, W6 0RX (8746 6888, www.101thaikitchen. com). Stamford Brook tube. Lunch served noon-3pm daily. Dinner served 6-10.30pm Mon-Thur, Sun; 6-11pm Fri, Sat. Main courses £6.50-£14.95.

69 Best burgers

Upmarket burger chain **Byron** has gone from strength to strength in recent years, and now has 25 branches in London – expect more to follow. Spaces are light, bright and attractive; staff are welcoming; and the burgers (from £6.75) are consistently great, with numerous toppings (bacon, avocado, roasted red pepper, portobello mushroom) and sauces (blue cheese, spicy BBQ, chipotle mayonnaise and so on) to keep customers coming back for more. **www.byronhamburgers.com**.

Dirty Burger has a rocking formula: cool junkyard-chic interiors courtesy of ultra-slick owner Soho House; reasonable prices; and exceptional cooking. A blend of carefully selected cuts goes into each patty, for a depth of flavour that, combined with pickles, cheese, lettuce, tomato and condiments, makes for a seriously good bite (cheeseburger £5.50). *79 Highgate Road, NW5 1TL (3310 2010, www.eatdirtyburger. com). Kentish Town tube. Open 7am-midnight Mon-Thur; 7am-1am Fri; 9am-1am Sat; 9am-11pm Sun.*

Honest Burgers Soho is the central London offshoot of the Brixton Market original (see p80). Try the £8 cheeseburger fashioned from 35-day dry-aged British chuck steak – courtesy of posh butcher Ginger Pig – topped with the likes of smoked bacon, sweet pickled cucumbers and slices of lip-smacking cheddar, red leicester or stilton. Mmmm. *4 Meard Street, W1F 0EF (3609 9524, www.honestburgers.co.uk). Leicester Square or Tottenham Court Road tube. Open noon-4pm, 5.30-11pm Mon-Thur; noon-11pm Fri, Sat; noon-10pm Sun.*

Meat Liquor (above) has a cult following for its grill-and-booze bar. Here, the sloppy, juicy burgers are knock-your-socks-off good. There's ground chuck steak in each one, and all manner of toppings available: chilli, mushrooms, bacon... Our favourite remains the Dead Hippie (£7.50), where two thin patties are anointed with melted cheese, tangy gherkins, finely diced onions and an addictive 'secret sauce'. See p64.

Mother Flipper serves burgers from a rickety market stall at various locations, including Brockley Market (Lewisham College Car Park, Lewisham Way, SE4 1UT, open 10am-2pm Sat). The quality of the food belies the humble setting. Soft, bouncy brioche buns are filled with 28-day-aged chuck beef, perfectly cooked and properly seasoned. Toppings run from the classic (pickles, lettuce, slices of US cheese) to the inspired (crisp pieces of streaky bacon 'candied' in brown sugar, or slices of hot-and-sweet pickled red jalapeños). Prices start at £5.50.
http://motherflipperburgers.com.

One of the newer burger bars is **Patty & Bun** in Marylebone. It's everything a cool burger bar should be, with hip (but super-friendly) staff, funky furnishings and a laid-back, reggae-infused vibe. The burgers (left) are insanely delicious and come with own-made mayos and relishes. Try the Smokey Robinson (£8), made with smokey P&B mayo, jammy caramelised onions and crisp bacon.
54 James Street, W1U 1HE (7487 3188, www.pattyandbun.co.uk). Bond Street tube. Open noon-10.15pm Tue-Sat; noon-9.15pm Sun.

Tommi's Burger Joint (below) is the first London opening for Tomas 'Tommi' Tómasson, an Icelandic restaurateur who owns a five-strong chain back home. Our top tip: the steak burger (£7.95, made with a higher grade of meat for a juicier patty), with a side of skinny fries.
58 Marylebone Lane, W1U 2NX (7935 5275, www.burgerjoint. co.uk). Bond Street tube. Open 11.30am-9.30pm Mon-Fri; noon-9.30pm Sat; noon-8pm Sun.

70 Panda Panda

The blissed-out bear logo and bright orange and white fittings make this a jolly lunchtime spot. The bright, clean interior also comes as a relief in a rather grimy part of town. Sandwiches, salads and smoothies employ colourful, fresh ingredients, as in vegetable rolls offset by a fiery chilli and peanut dipping sauce. The baguettes – used for the national sandwich of Vietnam (banh mi), or for mopping spicy beef soup – have a lovely light crunch thanks to the use of rice flour. Other hot options include noodle dishes and stews. Everything is beautifully presented, with artfully scattered chilli rings and parsley garnishes. Children get a shelf of picture books, and may also take a shine to Panda Panda's line in confectionery-based milkshakes. Adults will probably prefer the smoothies and fruit bubble teas. Smiley staff are super-efficient and happy to explain ingredients. Bring cash, as cards aren't accepted.

8 Deptford Broadway, SE8 4PA (8616 6922, http://panda-panda. co.uk). Deptford Bridge DLR or Deptford rail, or bus 177, 453. Open 10.30am-4.30pm daily. Main courses £1.99-£4.95.

71 Shepherdess Café

This landmark corner caff has appeared in several films and attracted a clutch of celebs in the three decades it's been open, but remains an unreconstructed greasy spoon, complete with eye-straining strip lighting, and old-fashioned plastic sauce bottles on each table. Classic full English breakfasts are the order of the day, with eggs, bacon, tomatoes and mushrooms costing £5.10; all manner of combos are available, with most plates arriving with chips (thick-cut, crispy but soft in the middle). Prices are similarly traditional: you'll pay just 80p for a cuppa here, while the (proper) coffee starts at £1.30 for an espresso. There's an extensive sandwich menu, and lunch dishes such as steak and kidney pie, and jacket potatoes. Have a peek at the photos on the luminous green wall behind the till – former customers include 1990s girl band All Saints, Barry from *EastEnders* and regular Jamie Oliver (his restaurant Fifteen is just round the corner).

221 City Road, EC1V 1JN (7253 2463). Old Street tube/rail.
Meals served 6.30am-4.30pm Mon-Fri; 7am-3pm Sat.
Main courses £5.40-£7.95.

72 Sagar

The Covent Garden outlet of this mini chain celebrates South Indian vegetarian specialities from the state of Karnataka. Furnishings are a restrained mix of blond wood, a few southern Indian ornaments, and wipe-clean tables. Dosais (rice and lentil pancakes) are some of the best in town, and star on the menu. For dramatic value, order a masala paper dosai, shaped into a gigantic hollow cone (almost 30cm at its widest point) and served with tart tamarind lentils (sambar), crushed potato and diced carrot masala mixed with fried curry leaves and mustard seeds, plus an astringent dollop of coconut and green chilli chutney. As well as southern specialities, such as the spongy, steamed rice dumplings (idlis), Sagar also covers Mumbai beach foods. Our favourite is pani poori: crisp pastry globes filled with tamarind water. There are branches in Hammersmith and Fitzrovia.

31 Catherine Street, WC2B 5JS (7836 6377, www.sagarveg.co.uk). Covent Garden tube. Meals served noon-11pm Mon-Sat; noon-10pm Sun. Main courses £5-£16. Set meal (noon-8pm) £5.95.

73 Fish & chips

While still one of Britain's favourite dishes, fish and chips is no longer the cheap supper it once was, and many of London's best-known chippies have long moved out of the budget league. Eating at the following establishments shouldn't leave you too out of pocket, however. All prices are for fish and chips, eaten on the premises.

In central London, special mention is due to the **Fryer's Delight** (19 Theobald's Road, WC1X 8SL, 7405 4114), an Italian-run chip shop that's been in business for over 40 years. Fish and chips starts at £4.75 (regular size £7.65), for fresh fish – chunky, firm and thinly coated in a light, flavoursome batter. What's more, there's no corkage charge (but no credit cards either). **Mr Fish** (9 Porchester Road, W2 5DP, 7229 4161, www.mrfish.uk.com) carries off its kitsch aquamarine decor and irony-free retro menu (avocado and prawns, scampi bites, spotted dick) with nostalgic charm. The place bustles with locals of every age, impressed by a broad choice of fish (including lemon sole, sea bass and rock – from £6.65) and moreish, chunky chips.

Sleek, modern **Kerbisher & Malt** (164 Shepherd's Bush Road, W6 7PB, 3556 0228, www.kerbisher.co.uk – right) brings the old-fashioned chip shop bang up to date, but still manages to offer fish and chips from £7.60. Fish is cooked to order, and can be battered, grilled or breaded;

most diners go for the traditional batter – a light, crispy coating. A sustainable approach means there's coley and pollock alongside haddock and cod. Such has been K&M's success that a new branch opened in Ealing in summer 2012.

Olley's (65-69 Norwood Road, SE24 9AA, 8671 8259, www.olleys.info) in Herne Hill is somewhere between the old and new in style, but is essentially a cracking, no-nonsense fish and chip restaurant, serving fat, crispy chips, epic fillets of a dozen types of fish (from £9.50 for a large portion), and big dollops of ice-cream for afters. South London is also blessed with **Something Fishy** (117-119 Lewisham High Street, SE13 6AT, 8852 7075) – an institution that's been serving hearty cooking at rock-bottom prices for longer than most locals can remember. The no-frills cafeteria counter is staffed by a troupe of cheery ladies, who dispense teas and coffees from an industrial-sized urn in the corner. Fish is cooked to order (from £4) and the batter is gloriously crisp.

In north London, **Sutton & Sons** (90 Stoke Newington High Street, N16 7NY, 7249 6444, www.suttonandsons.co.uk) is a friendly local chippy, serving ethically sourced fish (from its own fishmonger). The menu may feature loin of swordfish or half a dozen Maldon oysters, but Sutton's equally excels at classic cod and chips, with a deep golden crisp bubble around chunks of fresh white cod. Fish and chips cost from £6.90.

Since it opened more than 20 years ago, this backstreet grill has featured in every *Time Out Eating & Drinking Guide*. It's certainly doing something right to draw diners away from the numerous Turkish restaurants up and down Dalston's main drag – but it's far from flashy. The first thing you see on entering is the cabinet of skewers: cubed and minced lamb; chops and ribs; chicken wings and fillets; quail. There are even a few vegetables, though this is definitely a destination for meat eaters. Next to this display of flesh is the large charcoal grill, billowing smoke and overseen by a chef kept busy constantly twirling skewers and stoking the flames. Pretty much everything on the menu is worth ordering, but the beyti and adana kebabs (minced lamb) are particularly juicy and flavoursome, matched perfectly by fresh Turkish bread (free) and tart salad. Starters are fairly standard – meze, lahmacun and so on. There's no charge for BYO (although Mangal is licensed to sell alcohol), which, along with the good-value food, ensures the place is heaving most nights. Cash only.

10 Arcola Street, E8 2DJ (7275 8981, www.mangal1.com). Dalston Kingsland rail or 67, 76, 149, 243 bus. Lunch served noon-2.30pm, dinner served 6-10.30pm Mon-Sat. Main courses £6-£15.

75 | Spuntino

At lunchtime at least, the long queues that used to discourage visits to this no-phone, no-bookings and not-exactly-large retro American joint have dissipated. The lovely tiles behind the bar are original to the premises, a former butcher's shop, which partly alleviates the feeling you're in a theme restaurant: a carefully constructed London take on a New York take on road-food and Italian classics. In fact, you get some rather good-value (for the area), good-hearted cooking. Eggs receive a rare moment in the limelight: soft-boiled, on lentil and anchovy crostini; truffled, on toast; with soldiers; and in the best french toast this side of Chicago (if you like it sugar-sticky). Sliders amp up the flavour: pulled pork inauthentically but deliciously packs in crackling and pickled apple; bone marrow infiltrates ground beef. There are decent salads and desserts, and a mac 'n' cheese. Eat at stools at the bar or counters at the back (there are no tables as such).

61 Rupert Street, W1D 7PW (7734 4479, www.spuntino.co.uk).
Leicester Square or Piccadilly Circus tube. Meals served 11am-midnight Mon-Sat; noon-11pm Sun. Main courses £5.50-£10.

76 Little Georgia

While lacking the intimacy of the Hackney original, Islington's Little Georgia still stimulates interest in the under-documented culture of Georgia, with old telephones, traditional drinking horns and graphics-heavy political posters bringing originality to the otherwise standard jade green and cream interior. The menu is identical in both outlets (owner Tiko Tuskadze makes the dishes for the two restaurants in the N1 kitchen), and is a pleasing introduction to a cuisine that has influences from Europe and Asia. Cold starters include russian salad (a filling mix of potato, carrot, spring onion, pea, egg, dill and mayonnaise), while hot starters feature borscht and a baked-to-order khachapuri, a moreish cheese-filled bread that's a national staple. Homely mains – chashushuli (highly seasoned beef stew), kotnis lobio (a bean dish) and pan-fried poussin – are good too, especially on a cold night. Unlike the BYO Hackney branch, this place is licensed, with an extensive wine list. Georgian wine is very good, but if you're more in the mood for beer, then try one of the Russian lagers, such as Baltika.

14 Barnsbury Road, N1 0HB (7278 6100). Angel tube. Dinner served 7-11pm Tue-Fri. Meals served noon-11pm Sat, Sun. Main courses £8-£12.

77 Apollo Banana Leaf

The attractions here are threefold: a generous no-corkage BYO policy; recession-busting prices; and excellent cooking from Sri Lanka and South India. Short eats (street snacks) such as savoury lentil 'doughnuts' (vadais) or deep-fried, chilli-spiked fish cutlets are a good place to start, as are dosais (particularly the stuffed varieties), but the kitchen's true strength lies in its meat and fish curries. Mutton curry has tender meat in a deep, rich sauce with notes of fragrant cardamom. Tables are set far too close together, and service, though warm, can be slow, but this unassuming spot remains one of the area's brightest stars.

190 Tooting High Street, SW17 0SF (8696 1423, www.apollo bananaleaf.com). Tooting Broadway tube. Lunch served noon-3pm, dinner served 6-10.30pm Mon-Thur. Meals served noon-10.30pm Fri-Sun. Main courses £4.50-£9.

Historic Berwick Street Market, situated in the heart of Soho, has a handful of food stalls operating on weekdays (Monday can be pretty quiet, so visit from Tuesday for a wider choice of food). You should be able to pick up lunch for around a fiver; if it's a nice day, head to Soho Square to sit on the grass. The selection changes daily, but the following stalls are often present.

In addition to the delicious baguettes (above), pho soups and noodle salads from Vietnamese favourite **Banhmi11** (see p146), expect to find the **Pizza Pilgrims** (07780 667258, pizzapilgrims.co.uk), aka brothers James and Thom Elliott, who operate from the back of a tiny Piaggio Ape three-wheeler van – yes, there really is a pizza oven in there! With a crispy base and bubbling tomato and mozzarella topping, these pizzas look – and taste – like the real Neapolitan deal.

For real meaty goodness, the burgers from the **Tongue 'n Cheek** (07414 446545, www.tonguencheek.info) van deliver a choice of prime cuts of beef with cheddar, or pork belly with gorgonzola. Other offerings include falafel wraps from the suitably named **Jerusalem Falafel** (07411 128115), beef tagine from **Moroccan Box** (@moroccanbox), Mexican burritos from **Freebird Burritos** (see p66), Indian fare including curries, samosas and paneer wraps from **Tandoor**, and pork pies, sandwiches and cakes from the **Bread Man** (07815 601221).

Further south towards Shaftesbury Avenue, on Rupert Street, you'll find a smattering of other stalls, including **Somboon Thai Food**, which dispenses curries and noodle dishes.
*Berwick Street Market, between Broadwick Street
& Peter Street, W1.*

79 Bi Bim Bap

'We love bibimbap' – that's the message spelled out by hundreds of Polaroids of happy, smiling diners covering the white walls of this bright, modern eaterie. Rightly so, as bibimbap is the signature dish here, available in ten versions, including chilli chicken, mixed seafood and 'nutritious' (vegetables, chestnuts, dates, ginseng and ginkgo). White rice comes as standard, but brown is also available. Both are served in a sizzling stone bowl, with plastic bottles of koch'ujang and denjang sauces on the side, so that customers can mix the ingredients to their own satisfaction. The short menu also features some salads and noodle dishes, plus assorted sides, such as kimchi pancake, pork and vegetable dumplings, and miso soup. Drinks include Korean beer, plum wine, saké and ginseng tea. This isn't the place for a lingering meal, but it's ideal for a snappy lunch or dinner, with low prices and speedy service from young Korean staff.

11 Greek Street, W1D 4DJ (7287 3434, www.bibimbapsoho.com). Tottenham Court Road tube. Lunch served noon-2.30pm, dinner served 6-10.30pm Mon-Fri. Meals served noon-10.30pm Sat. Main courses £6.45-£9.95.

B-3 **seaside** ○
      noodle soup with Chinese cabbage   6.45

B-3 **tofu** ○   6.45
      soya tofu with mixed vegetables

B-4 **mixed mushroom** ○   7.95
      shiitake, white, oyster, black & vegetables

B-5 **nutritious** ○   8.45
      ginseng, ginkgo, dates, chestnut with vegetables
      served on a bed of brown rice

B-6 **chilli chicken**   6.95
      marinated in chilli, garlic and soy sauce with
      julienned vegetables

B-7 **beef bool-go-gi**   6.95
      specially marinated beef strips

80 Books for Cooks

One of London's more idiosyncratic eateries, Books for Cooks has a simple but very successful formula. From the small open kitchen, co-owner Eric Treuillé puts recipes (one starter, one main) from the cookbook(s) of the day to the test. There's no choice – until it comes to pudding, when there's an array of must-try cakes – but the standard of cooking is high. Lentil and pomegranate soup followed by beef and coconut curry is a typical lunch; cakes might include pear and raspberry, or the wonderfully moist flourless chocolate. White-wine lovers must go elsewhere: only red wine from Eric's own biodynamic vineyard is served (it's also available to take away, along with his olive oil). So popular is the bargain lunch in the tiny café at the back of this specialist cookbook shop that regulars start lurking from 11.45am to secure a table (no bookings are taken).

4 Blenheim Crescent, W11 1NN (7221 1992, www.booksforcooks. com). Ladbroke Grove tube. Open 10am-6pm Mon-Wed, Fri, Sat; 10am-5.30pm Thur. Lunch served noon-2pm (or until food runs out) Tue-Sat. Set lunch £5 2 courses, £7 3 courses.

81 Shoryu Ramen

Run by the same people as the Japan Centre across the road, Shoryu is an authentically Japanese experience. They've even shipped in a chef from Hakata, the district of Japan's Fukuoka city that's best known for the tonkotsu ramen in which the restaurant specialises. A good ramen has three key components: a well-flavoured broth, bouncy noodles and interesting toppings. The basic Hakata ramen here has a rich, milky, pork-and-chicken-bone broth with plenty of pale egg-yolk-yellow, own-made noodles crowned with slices of unremarkable barbecued pork, crunchy cloud ear mushrooms and slivers of bright red pickled ginger. The Hakata formula provides a base for variations such as the unusual wasabi ramen, which adds a topping of pickled wasabi stalks. If you're not in the mood for such a rich, creamy, meaty broth, there are miso or soy sauce (shoyu) alternatives. Note that bookings aren't taken.

9 Regent Street, SW1Y 4LR (7828 0747, www.shoryuramen.com). Piccadilly Circus tube. Lunch served noon-3pm, dinner served 5-10.30pm Mon-Fri. Meals served noon-10.30pm Sat. Main courses £8.50-£13.50.

While many of its contemporaries go out of their way to emulate the canteen feel of Tehran's downtown chelo kebab houses, Sufi is a restaurant in the conventional sense. This is one of the few places in London to capably blend authentic Persian cuisine with an intimate environment that's as suited to romantic liaisons as family reunions. The walls are hung with Middle Eastern musical instruments, calligraphic bronze art and the occasional framed painting of a wizened Sufi cleric. Candles illuminate the linen-clad tables after dark; and a traditional clay oven by the front door turns out soft and seeded taftoon bread. The latter makes a perfect accompaniment to a bowl of ash-e reshteh, a creamy noodle and bean soup. Kebabs are expertly grilled, but this is one place where it's worth experimenting: the khoresht-e fesenjan (chicken with chopped walnuts and pomegranate molasses) is flavourful, and there are some excellent fish and vegetarian dishes. The unusually decent wine list includes some punchy reds from Lebanon's Château Ksara, or you can BYO (corkage £5).

70 Askew Road, W12 9BJ (8834 4888, www.sufirestaurant.com).
Hammersmith tube then 266 bus. Meals served noon-10.45pm
daily. Main courses £7.30-£13.90.

83 Mosob

If you're familiar with Eritrean food, you're likely to enjoy Mosob – but if you're new to the cuisine, all the better. Service goes beyond cheery and attentive to positively educational, with a lesson in the communal eating style for all who need it. There are African and European beers and a decent cocktail list (including the 'sexy Mosob'), while the food centres on the staple that is injera: pleasingly sour, stretchy flatbread used to mop up meat stews, spiced split peas and vegetables. The well-priced set menus cover the most popular dishes, with ample choice for vegetarians. Starters of crispy falafel and veggie injera rolls make a great introduction, served with a fiery dip and yoghurt. Next comes a belt-busting platter of lamb, chicken, split pea and veg stews, served just as happily with rice and a fork for those who don't want to get hands-on. The meat is tender, the flavours fragrant and the textures deliciously varied. Service can be slow, and you're seated pretty close to other diners, but that's all the more reason to settle in for the night and make some new friends.

339 Harrow Road, W9 3RB (7266 2012, www.mosob. co.uk). Westbourne Park tube. Meals served 6-11.30pm Mon-Thur; 6-11.30pm Fri; 3-11.30pm Sat; 3-11pm Sun. Main courses £7.50-£12.95.

84 Mario's Café

Star of song (Saint Etienne's 1993 'Mario's Café') and screen (at the chrome counter you can buy a £3 DVD documentary about the caff), the café relies on locals' indefatigable appetite for cut-above breakfasts – scrambled egg and salmon, or poached egg and prosciutto, on ciabatta, a full English of sausage, egg, bacon and tomato, plus extras (bubble, hash browns, black pudding). But don't ignore the Italian mains – Mario's mum makes even a simple spicy Italian sausage penne delicious: decent ingredients, no fuss. Set among pretty pastel-painted cottages, the café is too narrow for comfort, but perfectly proportioned for bonhomie, which Mario dishes up as enthusiastically as the cappuccinos and nosh. It's a community place, with guitar lessons, doulas and t'ai chi lessons advertised, local art on the walls, and a steady stream of dads-with-nippers and retirees greeted by name. A true classic.

6 Kelly Street, NW1 8PH (7284 2066, www.marioscafe.com).
Kentish Town tube/rail. Meals served 7.30am-4pm Mon-Fri;
8am-4pm Sat. Main courses £5.50-£7.50.

Wembley? Surely that's for football? Well, yes, but it's also one of the best places in London for Indian food. The busy Ealing Road winds from Alperton tube north to Wembley High Road. It's less than a mile long, but it holds a seductive array of inexpensive restaurants serving dishes from across the subcontinent.

Leaving Alperton station, you'll soon encounter the sari shops, jewellery stores and cash 'n' carries that give the road its character. Since the 1970s, a wealth of people with south Asian ancestry – many from eastern Africa – have settled in the vicinity. Ealing Road is where they shop, pray (there's an ornate Hindu temple, a mosque and a Methodist chapel) and dine.

One of the first venues is also the most atypical: **Momo House** is a cosy little restaurant whose South African owner offers several unusual, sometimes challenging, Nepalese dishes (tooth-crackingly crunchy spiced soy beans called bhatmas, for instance) alongside the curry-house regulars. Try the succulent lamb momo dumplings. Across the road is **Maru's Bhajia House** (above), a favourite caff with African-Asian vegetarians, who chat over plates of mogo (cassava root) chips served with a thick tamarind dip.

Further on is **Asher's Africana**, a ludicrously cheap Gujarati vegetarian café. Note the 'Don't spit paan' window-sticker. Along with the crunchy snacks typical of this western Indian cuisine, there's a choice of thali set meals. The mini thali (gravy-like dahl, well-stocked vegetable curry, rice, yoghurt, onion salad and two chapatis) costs £3.50. If you hanker after meat, however, try neighbouring **Sohail's**, with its tawa (stir-fried), karahi and tandoori North Indian food.

Sakonis is an Ealing Road fixture, with crowds arriving at weekends for the vegetarian Gujarati buffets; at the front is a takeaway snack counter and a paan bar. After a lengthy residential interlude and then the Central Mosque, more shops and takeaways appear. **Kebabish** offers meaty North Indian karahis and kebabs in the dining room behind its takeaway counter.

South Indian and Sri Lankan cuisines soon make their presence felt. **Palm Beach** is the more upmarket Sri Lankan choice, where you can devour string hoppers accompanied by soothing music, though **Gana**, with its mutton liver curry and kothu rotis, has the more interesting menu.

Saravanaa Bhavan (right) opened in 2012: a suave addition to this international South Indian vegetarian chain, it serves Indo-Chinese snacks, biryanis and idlis plus well-constructed, satisfying thalis. You might well be enticed by the Dosa Express street stall just up the street, but Ealing Road's final flourish comes in the form of two chain vegetarian restaurants at the junction with Wembley High Road: **Sanghamam**, a popular meeting spot with its juice bar and South Indian, Mumbai chaat and Indo-Chinese menu; and purple-tinted **Chennai Dosa**, home to spicy South Indian pancakes.

Asher's Africana, 224 Ealing Road, HA0 4QL (8795 2455).
Chennai Dosa, 529 High Road, HA0 2DH (8782 2222, www.chennaidosa.com).
Gana, 24 Ealing Road, HA0 4TL (8903 7004).
Kebabish, 40 Ealing Road, HA0 4TL (8795 2656, www.kebabishoriginal.co.uk).
Maru's Bhajia House, 230 Ealing Road, HA0 4QL (8902 5570, 8903 6771).
Momo House, 2 Glenmore Parade, Ealing Road, HA0 4PJ (8902 2307, www.momohouse.co.uk).
Palm Beach, 17 Ealing Road, HA0 4AA (8900 8664, www.palmbeachuk.com).
Sakonis, 127-129 Ealing Road, HA0 4BP (8903 1058, www.sakonis.co.uk).
Sanghamam, 531-533 High Road, HA0 2DJ (8900 0777, www.sanghamam.co.uk).
Saravanaa Bhavan, 22 & 22A Ealing Road, HA0 4TL (8900 8526, www.saravanabhavan.com).
Sohail's, 238A Ealing Road, HA0 4QL (8903 6743).

86 | Wow Simply Japanese

This neat, cream-walled box of a restaurant conveys 'Japanese' with the simplest of ornamentation: two folk masks between the arched windows, and a straw saké keg over the door. The main menu looks more traditional than the fusion-leaning repertoire offered when Wow opened in 2006, though there's still a welcome preponderance of garlic, chilli and coriander. The pungent garlic and spring onion on our beef tataki tasted so good with the silky slivers of rare meat that we felt reluctant to use the accompanying ponzu. And the garlic rice rocks. The specials list seems less special now that it features such workaday dishes as tori kara age (deep-fried chicken) alongside sea bass carpaccio. However, the bottom line is attractive, with bento lunches costing under £10 and dinner comfortably inside the £25-a-head zone. And Wow seems to suit any type of diner: pairs of friends, groups, couples, the odd single, families at weekends. Staff don't always know their stuff, but service is comfortably paced. This being Crouch End, the wine list includes a couple of organic labels.

18 Crouch End Hill, N8 8AA (8340 4539, www.wowsimply japanese.co.uk). Finsbury Park tube/rail then bus W3 or W7, or Crouch Hill rail. Lunch served noon-2.30pm Wed-Sat. Dinner served 6-10.30pm Mon-Sat; 6-10pm Sun. Main courses £5.50-£15.20.

87 | Shanghai Dalston

At this long-running restaurant on Dalston's main drag, the tiles and fittings of a Victorian pie and mash shop meet a window display of hanging roast ducks, racks of ribs and crispy pork, plus a large Buddha and the usual accoutrements of a neighbourhood Chinese restaurant. Along with a menu of staples and a few more unusual dishes, dim sum is available all day. Execution can be variable, but in general the food is nicely presented and above the average high-street quality – a plate of duck and crispy pork on rice is a match for any similar dish in Chinatown. Two bookable karaoke rooms are a further incentive to dine here.
41 Kingsland High Street, E8 2JS (7254 2878, www.shanghai dalston.co.uk). Dalston Kingsland rail. Meals/dim sum served noon-11pm daily. Main courses £5.20-£10.60. Dim sum £2.80-£4.90.

88 Herman ze German

Head down Villiers Street, between the Strand and the Embankment, and on the left you'll see a quirky orange and white logo of a moustachioed sausage. Welcome to Herman ze German, the creation of a German couple homesick for their favourite sausages; after a couple of years touring music festivals with a street-food van, they opened this small shop. There are two wooden tables with stools, but it's really a takeaway joint. The  smooth-middled bockwurst is made from smoked pork, and has a firm casing giving it plenty of 'snap'. It's even tastier pimped with mild sauerkraut or crisp onions. Alternatives include bratwurst (pork and veal), chilli (beef and pork) and leberkäse (pork); all can be served in a baguette or as currywurst – chopped up, with a topping of sweetish curry-tomato sauce. You can also get fries and little pots of potato or carrot salad. To drink, there's Fritz-Kola and Chegworth Valley fruit juices, but no alcohol.

19 Villiers Street, WC2N 6NE (7839 5264, www.herman-ze-german. co.uk). Embankment tube or Charing Cross tube/rail. Meals served 7am-11pm Mon-Wed; 7am-11.30pm Thur; 7am-midnight Fri; 10am-11.30pm Sat, Sun. Dishes £4.25-£6.95.

89 Muya

The excellent-value food here is the equal of anything we've eaten in Addis Ababa. Kitfo – lean minced beef, briefly heated in spiced clarified butter and served almost raw, like steak tartare – comes topped with ayib, a soft cheese similar to ricotta. Also worth ordering are minchet abish alicha wot, a curry-like dish of finely ground beef flavoured with turmeric and ginger; and key wot, a spicy stew featuring tender lamb. Injera, the crumpet-like spongy bread, is served with every meal. Ethiopian drinks include reliable lagers Castel and St George's, though oenophiles won't be impressed by the rudimentary wine list. Service is friendly and informative, which goes some way to compensating for the dullness of the decor and the generic background music.

13 Brecknock Road, N7 0BL (3609 0702, www.muya restaurant.com). Kentish Town tube/rail or Camden Road rail. Dinner served 6-11pm Mon-Sat; 6-10pm Sun. Main courses £9.45-£16.50.

90 Franco Manca

One of the originators of Brixton's über-cool market scene, Franco Manca is a study in the importance of keeping it simple. The restaurant's Italian owner, Giuseppe Mascoli, pays homage to the best Neapolitan pizzerias, serving delicious slow-rise sourdough-crust pizzas that are topped with simple sauce, top-notch British-sourced, Italian-style cheese, cured meats and seasonal vegetables, and cooked for 40 seconds at high temperature in a brick oven. The classic margherita – tomato sauce, fresh mozzarella and basil – is perfectly executed. Alternatively, there's a choice of five other standard pizzas, as well as two daily specials. Like the food, the drinks list is well edited, and includes a handful of wines and beers along with Franco Manca's own refreshing lemonade. Great pizza at very reasonable prices means there's usually a queue (bookings are not accepted), but at least turnover tends to be rapid. Franco Manca's success has led to three other outlets, in Chiswick, Battersea and at Westfield Stratford City.

4 Market Row, Electric Lane, SW9 8LD (7738 3021, www.franco manca.co.uk). Brixton tube/rail. Lunch served noon-5pm Mon. Meals served noon-10.30pm Tue-Sun. Main courses £4.50-£6.95.

91 Imli

The emphasis at this offshoot of Mayfair restaurant Tamarind is on 'Indian tapas': small plates designed for sharing that focus on the subcontinent's varied street food. This means that bhel poori, papdi chat and coriander vada sit alongside more modern variants such as spicy battered squid, and tandoor-grilled meat, fish and vegetable dishes. There are special lunch deals, including nicely priced curry 'platters' and Indian sandwiches (aka 'naanwich'), a pre-theatre menu and usually a couple of special offers – check the website before you visit. In the main, it's good-value, competently executed food, if slightly dumbed down for western tastes. Decor similarly has a blandly corporate feel.

167-169 Wardour Street, W1F 8WR (7287 4243, www.imli.co.uk). Oxford Circus or Tottenham Court Road tube. Meals served noon-10.45pm Mon-Sat; noon-9.45pm Sun. Tapas £3.95-£10.95.

92 Mien Tay

Not much changes at family-run Mien Tay. It's still one of the least fancified restaurants in the Vietnamese enclave on Kingsland Road; decor could be generously described as 'homely', although more truthfully it's in sore need of a sprucing up. Service is still brisk, occasionally warm. But, reassuringly, the food is still brilliant: this remains one of the best (and best-value) places to eat Vietnamese in London. Do order the barbecued quail: a quartered and blackened bird, marinated in spices and honey, and served simply with a chilli and herb salad and aromatic dipping salt. The menu focuses on the cuisine of south-west Vietnam, although there are dishes from elsewhere: the pho is a fine version, if a bit too liberally speckled with sliced red onion. A speciality is the whole 'hard-fried' fish, served with green mango: perfect for picking over with chopsticks. The seafood hotpots are also popular. There's also a branch in Battersea, on Lavender Hill.

122 Kingsland Road, E2 8DP (7729 3074, www.mientay.co.uk).
Hoxton rail. Meals served noon-11pm Mon-Sat; noon-10pm Sun.
Main courses £6.50-£12.50.

93 Food for Thought

Celebrating its 40th birthday in 2014, Food for Thought is a phenomenon – still occupying the same cramped Neal Street premises, still serving an array of nourishing, flavourful grub at low prices, and still packed out every lunchtime. The pine furniture and chunky stoneware plates have a 1970s vibe too. The menu changes daily, offering soup, quiche, three hot mains – perhaps stir-fried veg with rice, or zingy cauliflower, spinach and pea curry – plus assorted salads, desserts and cakes. Vegan, wheat-free and gluten-free options are marked; portions are hefty (the scones – savoury and sweet versions – are almost indecently large). For takeaway, stay on the ground floor; to eat in, descend the steep stairs, order and pay for your food at the kitchen counter, and hope there'll be somewhere to sit. Neither bookings nor credit cards are accepted.

31 Neal Street, WC2H 9PR (7836 0239, www.foodforthought-london.co.uk). Covent Garden tube. Meals served noon-8pm Mon-Sat. Lunch served noon-5pm Sun. Main courses £4.20-£8.20.

Banhmi11 has become a weekday lunchtime fixture at Berwick Street Market. Crisp-shelled baguettes – **banh mi** – are filled with a choice of freshly grilled meats, fish or tofu and topped with carrot, daikon pickle, cucumber and coriander; prices start at £5. Our favourite is the Imperial BBQ, which mixes sweet caramelised barbecued pork with fresh lemongrass and coriander, and fish sauce, finished off with a kick of fiery chilli. Also look out for the stall at Broadway Market (Sat) and Chatsworth Road (Sun).
Banhmi11, Berwick Street Market, W1F 8TW (www.banhmi11.com). Open 11am-3pm Tue-Fri.

Bhangra Burger calls its **lamb wrap** with lime pickle the 'crazy lamb jalfrezi burger'. For £6.50, spice-marinated lamb mince is served with mango chutney, raita and sharp lime pickle, rolled up in a Lebanese khubz flatbread. Among the van's regular locations are Kerb (see p108), StockMKT in Bermondsey, and Street Feast in Shoreditch.
Bhangra Burger food van (07859 004628, www.bhangraburger.com).

Hot dogs were considered to be low-brow food until the **Big Apple Hot Dogs** (see p39) stall set up on an unlovely stretch of Old Street. Free-range pork, prime beef and judicious seasoning are used in custom-made sausages (from £3) that banish all thoughts of weak and watery canned wieners. Even the buns are baked in Hoxton (by Anderson's bakery). The signature sausage is the marjoram- and garlic-tinged Big Dog, a mix of pork and beef that's double smoked over German beechwood.

Join a salivating queue for the renowned **chorizo buns** served by Spanish food importer **Brindisa** from the stall outside their Borough Market shop. For a very reasonable £3.75 (£4.95 if you want two pieces of chorizo), enjoy freshly grilled sausage oozing piquant paprika oil, plus silky piquillo red pepper and peppery rocket, all stuffed inside a toasted ciabatta roll.

Brindisa stall, Borough Market, 18-20 Southwark Street, SE1 1TJ (www.brindisa.com). Open noon-2.15pm Tue, Wed; noon-3pm Thur; noon-4pm Fri; noon-5pm Sat.

Street food at its messy best, Arturo Ortega Rodriguez's **tacos** (£2.50 for one, £6 for three), are as close to the real deal as you'll get in London. In the Yucatán-style cochinita pibil, juicy pork comes marinated in orange juice with achiote (a red-coloured seed) for that deep burnished colour. You can load up your taco with as much salsa and guacamole as you like – the combination of the meat with added chilli, sweet red onion, tomatoes, lime and roughly crushed avocado makes for an explosive mouthful.

Buen Provecho, Lower Marsh, SE1 7RG (07908 210311, www.buenprovechomc.com). Open 11am-2.30pm Mon-Fri.

We like **Jerk City** (see p20) for its home-style Caribbean dishes, many of which are Trinidadian and influenced by the island's Asian population. The **mutton roti** (£7) is a case in point, with its generous portion of thick, flaky flatbread and peppery, spicy curried mutton. Many customers order food to take away, but there's a smattering of wooden tables if you want to eat in. Service can be haphazard, so try to avoid the lunchtime rush.

Relive the backpacker experience at **KaoSarn**, a bargain-priced Thai café in Brixton Village Market. The **som tam** (green papaya salad, £5.50) is just like the street vendors in Thailand would make it – complete with slivers of bird's-eye chilli that assault your palate with their heat. The sharp citrus crunch of green papaya is given sour notes by the addition of ground dried shrimps, with crushed peanuts adding nuttiness.

KaoSarn, Brixton Village Market, Coldharbour Lane, SW9 8PR (7095 8922). Open noon-3.30pm, 5.30-10pm Tue-Sun.

95 Ariana II

A cosy little local with a plate-glass window, behind which Afghan tassels and framed photos adorn a simple dining area featuring black tiled flooring, brick walls and dark furniture. Sweet, enthusiastic and swift service brightens proceedings, as does the multicultural bunch of regulars – and the food. In addition to a raft of appetising-looking kebabs, the long menu holds plenty that is singularly Afghan. Start with tangy aushak: delicate ravioli parcels filled with leeks, smothered in a tomato and mince sauce and dribbled with yoghurt, accompanied by a mint, chilli and lemon relish. Follow this with kabuli palow: a monumental mound of fluffy rice covering an entire, tender lamb shank, topped with sweet red strips of carrot, raisins and nuts, with a side dish of stewed kidney beans. Puddings also negotiate a line between the Middle East (baklava) and India (firnee, a yoghurt and nut confection). Low prices and a BYO policy (no corkage) increase the appeal.

241 Kilburn High Road, NW6 7JN (3490 6709, www.ariana2 restaurant.co.uk). Kilburn tube or Brondesbury rail. Meals served noon-11pm daily. Main courses £6-£12.

96 | Lahore Kebab House

LKH dishes out generous portions of brilliantly bold Punjabi grills, snacks and curries, and has been doing so for decades. A recent expansion has eased some of the queues that form on weekend evenings. Diners come for rich, powerfully spiced dahls and meat curries (some on the bone), piles of sweet onion bhajia, fiery grilled lamb chops and seekh kebabs, and fresh breads dripping with ghee. Everything is served in a rustic fashion, often in karahi on utilitarian metal stands, in keeping with the spartan (and spick-and-span) surroundings. It's not the kind of restaurant to take a date: large groups descend to take advantage of the bargain prices and BYO policy (corkage no charge), and flatscreen TVs distract with IPL matches or Bollywood films. But for authentically vivid flavours in a no-nonsense setting, Lahore is hard to beat.

2 Umberston Street, E1 1PY (7488 2551, www.lahore-kebabhouse. com). Aldgate East or Whitechapel tube. Meals served noon-midnight daily. Main courses £6-£10.50.

97 | Seoul Bakery

At £3.50, you'd be hard pushed to find a cheaper bibimbap in London than the one on offer at this Korean caff tucked behind Centre Point, amid a row of other Korean restaurants. Pay an extra quid and they'll add some beef, chicken or tuna to the rice, fried egg, vegetable and chilli sauce combo. Other highlights of the classic Korean menu are generously proportioned seafood pajeon pancakes – not the crispest, but guaranteed to fill you up – and fried rice dishes or spicy stews with boiled rice for around a fiver. The diminutive dining room, covered in cutesie Post-it note messages and doodles from diners, is often packed with students looking for a bargain-priced meal – you may well have to queue to get in. Note that it's cash only.

55 St Giles High Street, WC2H 8LH (no phone). Tottenham Court Road tube. Meals served noon-11pm daily. Main courses £3.50-£5.99.

You can easily spot London's favourite Japanese noodle bar by the long queue regularly winding from its entrance (no bookings are taken). Fear not – there's a fairly rapid turnover at the shared wooden tables, and the food (authentic Japanese preparations using fresh, locally sourced vegetables, meats and fish) is worth the wait. The menu stars udon noodles (chewy, thick white noodles made with wheat flour imported from Japan) in all their glorious possibilities: hot in soup, cold and served with hot soup, or cold served with cold sauce. There are also rice dishes and an impressive list of salads and sides. Seasonal specials, listed on a blackboard, often feature more exotic combinations than the regular menu. Koya's own ginger tea makes an ideal accompaniment to the salty food. Friendly staff can guide you through the dishes.

49 Frith Street, W1D 4SG (7434 4463, www.koya.co.uk).
Tottenham Court Road tube. Lunch served noon-3pm daily.
Dinner served 5.30-10.30pm Mon-Sat; 5.30-10pm Sun.
Main courses £6.90-£14.30.

99 Maoz

This fast-food joint, specialising in freshly deep-fried falafel, is handily located in the heart of Soho and opens late. Order one of the several set-meal options and you can then fill the remaining space in your pitta bread (white or wholemeal) with a selection of the crisp salads from the well-stocked salad counter – we particularly like the pickled aubergine. Then help yourself to the dispensers providing herbed yoghurt dressing, mayonnaise or ketchup. The chips are excellent too: fat, firm and golden. We can recommend the own-made lemonade, which is simple but good. Although there are a few tables, Maoz is not a place to linger. But the food is consistently good, entirely vegetarian, and very filling if you don't want to spend a lot.

43 Old Compton Street, W1D 6HG (7851 1586, www.maozusa.com). Open 11am-1am Mon-Thur; 11am-2am Fri, Sat; 11am-midnight Sun. Main courses £4.40-£6.50.

STEP 1 CHOOSE YOUR BASE		Sel Out	Eat In
1 Falafel in Pitta		4.40	5.40
Salad Pitta Falafel Balls Self service salad & sauce			
2 Falafel in Box		5.30	6.30
Salad in box - Pitta Falafel Balls Self service salad & sauce			
3 Salad Pitta		4.50	5.50
Salad Bar Items Only			
4 Salad Box		4.20	5.20
Salad Bar Items Only			
5 Fresh Chips		2.10	2.60

STEP 2 CHOOSE YOUR EXTRAS		
1 Hummus	0.50	0.60
2 Aubergine	0.50	0.60
3 Feta Cheese	0.50	0.60
4 Babaganoush	0.50	0.60
5 Avocado	0.50	0.60
6 Boiled Egg	0.50	0.60
7 Mozzarella	0.50	0.60

All salad bar items are self service, one visit to the s...

gluten free falafel

100 E Pellicci

You go to Pellicci's as much to dine on the atmosphere as the food. Opened in 1900, and still in the hands of the same family, this Bethnal Green landmark has an almost-opulent appearance that conjures up some mythical caff culture where the spoons were silver rather than greasy. The decor – chrome and Vitrolite outside; wood panelling with deco marquetry, Formica tabletops and stained glass within – earned the café a Grade II listing in 2005. The food (steadfastly quotidian) is prepared with pride by Mamma Maria, queen of the kitchen since 1961. Her children, Anna and Nevio Junior, serve it up with a wink. Recommended are the fry-ups, spaghetti 'Toscana', Friday fish 'n' chips, and desserts from bread pudding to Portuguese pasteis de nata. You can't book, and it's cash only.

332 Bethnal Green Road, E2 0AG (7739 4873). Bethnal Green tube/rail or bus 8. Meals served 7am-4pm Mon-Sat. Main courses £6.60-£8.40.

The numbers below refer to **page numbers**.

Cuisine Index

Area Index